THE LANGUAGE OF FEELINGS

Also by David Viscott

HOW TO LIVE WITH ANOTHER PERSON
THE MAKING OF A PSYCHIATRIST
DORCHESTER BOY

THE LANGUAGE
OF FEELINGS

by David Viscott, M. D.

PRIAM BOOKS

ARBOR HOUSE

NEW YORK

Library of Congress Catalogue Card Number: 75-40511
ISBN: 0-87795-130-6
Manufactured in the United States of America

Priam Trade Paper Edition: 0-87795-525-5

10 9 8 7 6 5 4 3 2 1

For Kathy

Acknowledgments

THE AUTHOR wishes to thank Ms. Jayne Chamberlin for her help in organizing the preliminary notes for this manuscript. The author is deeply indebted to Donald Fine his publisher and editor for the care and patience he showed in working with a most difficult book.

Contents

Author's Note

OUR FEELINGS are our sixth sense, the sense that interprets, arranges, directs and summarizes the other five. Feelings tell us whether what we experience is threatening, painful, regretful, sad or joyous. Feelings can be described and explained in simple and direct ways. There is nothing mystical or magical about them. Feelings make up a language all their own. When feelings speak, we are compelled to listen—and sometimes act—even if we do not always understand why. Not to be aware of one's feelings, not to understand them or know how to use or express them is worse than being blind, deaf or paralyzed. Not to feel is not to be alive. More than anything else feelings make us human. Feelings make us all kindred.

Feelings are our reaction to what we perceive, and in turn they color and define our perception of the world. Feelings, in fact, *are* the world we live in. Because so much of what we know depends upon our feelings, to be awash in confusing or dimly perceived feelings is to be overwhelmed by a confusing world.

My purpose in writing this book is to explain the nature of feelings—what they mean, how they work, where they come from, and how to understand and use them. The explanation I offer here is derived as much from my training and experience in practice as it is from my familiarity with and understanding of myself, which, though incomplete, is hopefully still growing. In developing my perspective I've become more aware of my own limitations, and have tried to take care to see that they don't intrude. I do not pretend to have all the answers. I have, though, gained a certain knowledge of feelings over the years, and I'll attempt to set down these insights in as direct and simple a manner as possible.

The language of feelings is the means by which we relate with ourselves, and if we cannot communicate with ourselves we simply cannot communicate with others. As I've said, we perceive the world through our five senses. The sensory impressions thereby relayed to us must be integrated anew by each of us. How each of us perceives with any given sense varies, but not nearly as much as how each of us "makes sense" of the world he perceives. This process of integrating the world in our own fashion is a basic mental process. It is also the creative process.

Our feelings are our reaction to what we have perceived through the senses and they shape our reaction to what we will experience in the future.

A person who carries much unsettled anger around with him, for example, is likely to find the world he encounters to be also angry and so justify and perpetuate his own feeling of anger.

I believe this suggests that the world is largely one of our own creation. In fact the world *is* considerably more under our influence than most of us realize. When a person assumes responsibility for his feelings, he also assumes responsibility for his world. Understanding feelings is the key to mastery of ourselves, finding true independence, which is to attain the only real power worth having. While this idea implies that each of us is on his own, it also means that there's much that each of us can do to set straight the disjointed pieces of his life and bring them into harmony. Indeed, I suspect if each person accepted the responsibility for putting his own emotional world in order, the larger world might also become more real, harmonious and even peaceful.

I hope this book will help to take some of the mystery out of feelings, to make it more possible for people to recognize and understand what they feel, to show where their feelings come from and where they are going so that they can be an ally—instead of an enemy—to their own natural progression. I don't propose any flashy, modish way for doing this. Understanding is the basic method, and my hope is that through it each reader will feel a new awareness of himself.

There's probably much in these pages that nearly everyone has thought, at least felt, before. This book attempts to put this in some order and thereby make it more useful — to indicate a language of feelings and thereby articulate a syntax of the emotions.

As people become more open with their feelings there's less need to guard against things in the world that are threatening; for instead of hiding from feelings, the open person uses them as a guide that interprets the world he is experiencing. People who rely solely on their intellect to find their way through the world are not as likely to be as in harmony as people who also use their feelings. The highest accomplishments of man are not in the precision of his science, but in the perfection of his art. Man's art is the celebration of his feelings at their most coherent point.

Reality can't be comprehended without taking into account feelings. The abstractions of intellect and reasoning are important, but when they lose touch with feelings they open the way for inhuman and destructive acts. When we lose touch with our feelings, we lose touch with our most human qualities. Living in our feelings, we are most in touch, most alive. To paraphrase Descartes, there is nothing more true than "I feel, therefore, I am."

In this book I hope to construct a framework against which the reader can examine his own feelings and his life. In so doing I also hope to offer a guide for allowing feelings to find their most natural expression in as economical and socially acceptable a manner as possible and in the process have the best likelihood of resolving conflicts and encouraging growth. Our feelings can be managed defensively or creatively, the one a turning inward, the other an expressive flowing outward.

All this, I realize, is a very large order indeed, and one that at best can only be incompletely filled. The reader, I hope, will take the ideas and methods suggested here and use them as he sees fit to work out the riddle, assembling the details of his own experience and from them creating his own best life by and for himself.

DAVID VISCOTT

since feeling is first
who pays any attention
to the syntax of things
will never wholly kiss you;
   —e e cummings

CHAPTER ONE

Feelings

FEELINGS ARE the way we perceive ourselves. Feelings are our reaction to the world around us. They are the way we sense being alive. When our feelings are settled we experience our highest consciousness. Without feelings there is no existence, no life. Put simply, each of us *is* his feelings. What we feel about anything reflects our history and development, our past influences, our present turmoil and our future potential. To understand our feelings is to understand our reaction to the world around us.

Without an awareness of what our feelings mean, there is no *real* awareness of life. Our feelings summarize what we have experienced and tell us if it is pleasurable or painful. No two people have the same way of integrating what they perceive. The reality we derive from our perceptions is largely a creation of our own needs and expectations. Even so, there are common ways in which each of us deals with his reaction to his experience — his feelings. No matter how we assemble the fragments of this world into our outlook, there are universal patterns to feelings, and these reactions are predictable and easily understood.

While each of us may differ in what he thinks is important, we are all much alike in the way we react, for example, to an important loss. When the human experience is reduced to such basic feelings, it's possible to have compassion for others, because feelings make all mankind kindred. When we begin to understand this, many of the mysteries of life evaporate.

Feelings are the most direct reaction to our perception. When we use words alone to describe what we perceive we are really attempting to manage our feelings rather than experience them. Thinking is a much more indirect way of handling reality than feeling. Feelings tell us when something is painful and hurts, because feelings *are* the hurt. Thought explains the hurt, justifying, rationalizing, putting it into perspective.

The most intelligent of men have no particular advantage over others in understanding what they feel. Indeed a high intelligence is often a severe handicap when it is used to rationalize feelings and offer logical, but none the less elusive, detours away from the truth. Everyone knows intelligent people who do not seem to have any understanding of their feelings, and as a result make poor and untrustworthy companions. They distort the world, although at times with a convincing elegance and even grace, but still remain far from understanding themselves. Such people seem to function best within the narrow confines of their intellectual system, which provides them with a safe corner from which they can view the world, comment upon it knowingly and yet remain outside the mainstream of human feeling. These people have focused on one aspect of human growth, the ordering of detail by logic.

In this intellectual sphere defenses are formed. Words are used instead of feelings. The world is created two-dimensionally out of concepts, and feelings are not trusted because they are, literally, so disarming.

The world is so complicated that we can't rely solely on our intellectual capacity to evaluate our perceptions. We perceive a large number of stimuli and must hunt for the common denominator. Our ability to think lets us form concepts and classify our impressions. But fortunately there are shortcuts in the mental process and the most easily understood link between outside stimuli and the impressions we perceive is a feeling. For example, we may experience a sudden fear warning us our survival is being threatened long before we are able to form a mental concept that brings us to the same conclusion. Sometimes, though, we allow our feelings to color our perceptions. While this may make us more alert and more self-protective, it can also distort the world we perceive — particularly when it makes us feel overly vulnerable to it.

The world is a puzzle each of us assembles differently. But each of us can learn to deal with it by using our natural gifts in a more effective way—which includes learning to feel more honestly. The more honest you become the more energy you will have to deal with the problems you face. Being in touch with your feelings is the only way you can ever become your highest self, the only way you can become open and free, the only way you can become your own person. Seeing the world intellectually is as different from "feeling" it as studying a country in a geography book is from living there.

If you don't live in your feelings, you don't live in the real world. Feelings are the truth. What you do with them will decide whether you live in honesty or by a lie. Using defenses to try to manage feelings may distort your perception of the truth, but it does not alter that truth. Explaining feelings away does not resolve them or exorcise them. They're there. They have to be dealt with. Putting the blame on others does not take away their sting, or reduce their intensity. Feelings may be disguised, denied, rationalized, but a painful feeling will not go away until it has run its natural course. In fact when a feeling is avoided, its painful effects are often prolonged and it becomes increasingly difficult to deal with it.

To understand the emotional and psychological effects of pain it's helpful to understand its physical nature. Physiologically the sensation of pain is transmitted through specific nerve fibers and is perceived when any sensory receptor is overloaded beyond its normal capacity to receive and transmit information. When pressure becomes too severe or temperature too hot, or sound too loud the stimulus is no longer perceived as pressure, temperature or sound, but as pain. An electrical current, called the current of injury, is initiated in the nerve ending and is sent along to the brain. The painful impulse produces an avoidance response that causes us to remove the threatened part of the body from danger—a reaction that often occurs automatically.

This avoidance response is basic to the understanding of human feelings, because painful human feelings also produce a current of injury, telling us that we are in danger and that we must protect ourselves. Feelings can be overloaded just as any other energy system can.

When an emotional injury threatens, our natural reaction is to avoid it. If the injury is not avoidable, it should be accepted as a real threat in order to make preparations to reduce the extent of the injury so the best remedy can be decided on. Just as during the development of the child's independent striving, so too in the process of injury and healing there is a time for support and assistance and a time when a person by himself must help along the process of healing, which is also a period of growth.

Sometimes, though, we overreact to painful

feelings and set up impenetrable defenses. When our feelings are altered by such defenses, separating us from pain, managing feelings can become difficult because we simply lose sight of the problem.

There is a time for defenses and a time when they should be put aside. The purpose of defenses is to protect against further injury by giving us some distance and time. When they are used too broadly to shield us from all pain, they use so much energy they have nearly the same depleting effect as the injury itself. The energy that's consumed by defenses goes into putting up and maintaining a barrier to reality. Each of us needs to find a balance between pain and defense and rely on his own experience as a guide. While we frequently have little choice whether to use a defense or not, we can lower our defenses by enduring as much pain as we can tolerate until most of the pain is gone. It's not easy, it takes courage, but it works.

Basically there are two general kinds of feelings, positive and negative. Positive feelings add to one's sense of strength and well being, producing pleasure, a sense of completion, life, fullness and hope. Negative feelings interfere with pleasure, use up energy and leave one drained, with a sense of truncation, emptiness and loneliness. Positive feelings are joyous, like the sexual expressions between two people who care for each other or like the feeling of being reunited with a friend or achieving a hard-sought goal. Negative feelings have the impact of loss, like the perception of little deaths everywhere one looks. Positive feelings often find their expression in creative works, such as a work of art or a new idea. Positive feelings can also be an act of love or kindness. They have a sense of renewal about them.

The purpose of understanding your feelings and allowing them to flow to their natural conclusion is to become as open and as free of negative feelings as possible so that you can become your higher, more creative and productive self. Higher, because you are increasingly free of the burden of defenses that have their roots in fear and pain. More creative, because your energy is being expressed outwardly in a positive way, enhancing whatever it comes in contact with in your own unique way. More productive, because your energies are no longer drained by the need to keep feelings from being expressed, and you gain strength by expressing them in a natural way.

When you suffer the emotional injuries that everyone occasionally must, you may be drained of energy and feel hurt and hopeless for a time. This is a natural result of being injured. If you allow yourself to experience the natural stages of emotional hurt without trying to avoid reality you will be able to resolve your pain more completely. Your energy will return sooner and with it your creativity and productiveness.

Feelings should reflect the present and provide a personal perspective on the events you are confronting. This doesn't mean there's no room in the present for memories of happy times or sad events. Rather it means that feelings should be derived primarily from what is happening now, not from the unsettled events of the past. Which is why, of course, we should try to settle the pain of the past and be free to look back at the details of our lives from the perspective of understanding—which opens the way to continuing growth. The past should not be bound down in a rigid memory that has been defensively maintained, for example, to support a favorable impression of ourselves. When we block out the parts of the past that are unflattering or embarrassing, we often lose more than we bargained for. The defenses that block unpleasant memories also block pleasurable ones. And that inability to remember what's positive robs us of energy and joy, and prevents us from forming and keeping an optimistic attitude. The ideal is to be free of the need to distort reality, so that if you wish you can recall feelings from the past and be free to reexamine them and settle them anew.

This process of solving emotional problems throughout life makes possible real growth and development. The developmental "issues" of childhood, for example, constantly reappear as conflicts in our lives and continue to shape us. If we remain open we can continue to grow. If we are closed and defensive, we waste our energy and never realize our potential. The issue of the earliest phase of development is dependency; the life goal is to achieve independence. The issue of the next phase is mastery and control; the life goal is to achieve freedom. The issue of the next phase is identity, including sexual; the life goal is simply to be comfortable being yourself and accepting your feelings without pretense.

Adolescence is the first opportunity to work through these earlier issues again, a chance to test the validity of previous conceptions, the strength of earlier defenses. It's also a time to reconsider compromises made out of fear of losing one's parents' love, out of fear of losing control of one's emotions, or out of fear of embarrassment. Typically adolescents display a wide and constantly varying pattern of defenses, bewildering the people around them by changing their stand on issues as well as self-image from one moment to the next. The adolescent is confronted with all of the lessons he was supposed to have mastered long ago—or at least that his parents *expected* him to have mastered. No wonder he seems bewildered.

As an adolescent's emerging sexual energies begin to seek expression they also tend to make him feel out of control. They create feelings and fantasies he may not find acceptable and he may act in a self-destructive way to punish himself. The adolescent sometimes feels crazy and often acts it. The classical picture of adolescent turmoil is all too familiar with its mood swings and acting out of feelings rather than "feeling" them.

The adolescent's behavior is his language for expressing his feelings. It's as valid for him as "talking out" feelings is for an adult. When a parent panics in the face of his adolescent's rebellion, he tends to reinforce his child's worst fears about himself. The parent then seems out of control to the adolescent, who now may believe *no one* can help him, and this can lead to severe testing of limits and encounters with the law.

Parents often try to quash feelings in their children that they feel uncomfortable about in themselves. Their dishonesty in refusing to admit their own feelings may make their child rebel even more—he can see through, or sense, their "adult" defense.

Some parents actually secretly encourage their children's acting up and live a life of vicarious fulfillment as their children do things they wish they'd had the courage to do either when they were adolescents themselves or at the very moment. A parent who feels trapped in a marriage, for example, may encourage his child to run away and then follow him in fantasy.

Just as adolescence provides a second chance for the child to master the unsettled issues of his earlier life, it often stirs up a second adolescence in the parent: The child may not only, as they say, be father to the man within, but to the parent without as well.

Try to keep in mind: If you don't treat your children's feelings as important, how can you expect them to act in their own best interests, which is in the best expression of their feelings? Postponing a child's assumption of responsibility for his own behavior and prematurely forcing that responsibility both cause problems — of seething anger and feeling stifled on the one hand, and feeling abandoned and overwhelmed on the other.

It's been said that an adolescent is grown up when he can do what he wants even if his parents are in favor of it. Good parents don't make that choice even more difficult by being opposed to something their children desire merely because they are afraid of their own feelings.

In the years that follow adolescence, the issues of the past continue to be brought up and at least partially resolved as age takes away the defenses of even the strongest resistance. In later years there is no use lying. The mirror tells the truth and we must accept it. This is not necessarily some painful "coming to grips" with things; it also means learning to enjoy what *pleases* us. Too bad we didn't know earlier what we know now about ourselves— that we are what we are and have been that all along. How difficult it is to learn simply to be.

Except how do we learn to be? By opening

ourselves to feelings. And how do feelings function? What is the natural process by which they make themselves manifest? Let's briefly take an example. Begin with anxiety. It's a negative feeling, but as we've seen, negative feelings can be turned to positive results if we know how to deal with them.

Anxiety is the fear of a hurt or a loss, either real or imagined, which has not yet occurred or has occurred but has not been fully accepted.

When a person experiences a hurt or a loss he feels pain.

Pain creates an imbalance and demands a response of energy. That corrective response needs to be directed outward at the source of the pain. The expression of that energy is called anger.

If that energy cannot be expressed outwardly as anger but instead is turned inward against the self, it's perceived as guilt.

If this guilt isn't soon relieved by accepting the original anger as a reasonable response to the original hurt, it's turned against the person feeling it. The guilt deepens and becomes depression. Such depression can destroy the person and consume all his energy.

ANXIETY IS THE FEAR OF HURT OR LOSS.
HURT OR LOSS LEADS TO ANGER.
ANGER HELD IN LEADS TO GUILT.
GUILT, UNRELIEVED, LEADS TO DEPRESSION.

Such feelings flow naturally when you suffer a loss. There are three major kinds of loss: the loss of someone who loves you or the loss of their love or your sense of lovability; the loss of control; the loss of self-esteem. Each particular sensitivity to loss originates in a specific developmental phase of early childhood. Of course everyone is sensitive to all of these losses — love, control and self-esteem — but when a person is especially sensitive to one type of loss he tends to use a certain set of defenses in managing that loss. The person who dreads being out of control, for example, sees the world in terms of control. He responds to every loss as if it were a reflection of his personal lack of control. In a similar fashion other people interpret all losses as proof that they are unlovable and some see all losses in terms of diminished personal esteem.

I'll talk about these three types of loss in more detail later, but in general, how you perceive a loss depends on where you stand in your own emotional development.

Common to all of these personal distortions of loss is the conviction that one simply must be perfect. We decide it's our own imperfections, which we usually have difficulty admitting to, that are responsible for our hurt. If we think we're at fault, but can't really admit it, we're likely to go through life trying to prove we're without flaws.

None of us, obviously, is without flaws, but it's much healthier to face up to them and learn how to deal with them than to deny their existence. At the same time, each of us is responsible for living the best—which is to say the fullest—life we're capable of. I realize that responsibility may be frightening to someone who has always avoided it, but it's also very freeing once you've really embraced the idea.

Who else but you would you trust with the responsibility for your feelings—your life?

Who but you could possibly know what you truly feel—especially if you don't know yourself? Other people may make educated guesses about your feelings, but the responsibility for *your* journey through this world is in *your own* hands. It always has been. It always will be.

It's in the country of feelings where the mistakes of the past and the problems of future growth have the greatest chance for being worked out anew. Issues that seem trapped, and defenses that seem rigid can often be made to flow once more so that each of us can progress from injury to healing, from pain to comfort, from fantasy and defense to reality and acceptance.

By learning to allow feelings to flow naturally, the world each of us perceives can also change and become more real, and we can become more accurate, more *honest*, in the way we feel about it. Without this there's not likely to be much happiness or fulfillment. Life is going to be wasted trying to be something other than your highest— your truest—self.

Don't be afraid to be yourself, to stand behind your feelings without pretending they are unimportant.

What is that self? Who are you? You are the person experiencing your feelings, creating your world.

CHAPTER TWO

Hurt and Loss

HURT is also known as being upset. Being upset is a catch-all expression used to describe all sorts of feelings without admitting very much.

As I sketched out in the previous chapter, people are hurt when they feel they have lost something. The more important the loss, the deeper the hurt. Often people are not aware how important something is to them until they lose it. The defenses that help a person deal with the world do so in large part by shielding him from vulnerability to loss.

Everyone feels vulnerable about something and no one feels totally secure. Accepting vulnerability instead of trying to hide it is the best way of adapting to reality. If you go through life pretending you can't be hurt, or that you can only be hurt by a set limited number of losses, you're doing more than fooling yourself. You're selling yourself short. To say that you can't be hurt is another way of saying you don't really care about yourself, your world or the people in it. If you're not vulnerable to loss, your investment in the world probably isn't very deep.

People who form only superficial ties are usually terrified of getting close to others. They fear to be abandoned, betrayed or rejected, even though their outward lifestyle may give others the impression there's nothing that would ever bother them. If someone has designed a lifestyle as a moat against involvement, you can be fairly sure there's little pleasure in that person's life — anything that acts as a rigid defense keeps out joy as well as pain. Rigidly defended people often live in a world that appears bland and colorless, offers little excitement or variety. So much is screened out by their defenses that their gray and boring perception of the world becomes self-perpetuating. Joy is opposite to hurt. Instead of something being depleted something fulfilling is given. People who can't accept hurt usually can't give pleasure. Both require openness. To be open means to be vulnerable—to be able to feel hurt, and to give pleasure.

Everyone has experienced hurt in his life. Often the losses most obvious even to a casual observer are difficult for us to acknowledge because we hurt most especially where our defenses operate. Discovering what a loss means to you is the first step in understanding the pain of hurt, and overcoming it.

Children tend to feel insecure and vulnerable because they're small and relatively helpless and dependent on someone else's strength. They have to be on good terms with their benefactor, which implies not doing anything that would take away from their protective relationship. Young people don't feel like their own persons. They don't feel they can be themselves without some risk of losing their protection. In growing up we learn that no matter how powerful the person who protected us happened to be, he couldn't always be counted on to protect us, and even if he could, he didn't always know what it was we felt threatened *by*, what to protect us *from*.

The childlike condition of being vulnerable also implies being open. But this condition can't long be endured by most people without their soon becoming defensive. We prefer to be protected rather than risk being open to hurt. In order to accept vulnerability without becoming defensive, you need a basic belief in your own goodness and inner strength, a belief that no matter what comes your way somehow you will manage. You also need to realize that whatever your faults are they're not especially unique, not much different from anyone else's. Also not nearly as bad as you thought. When you have the chance to exchange views and experiences with others, you find there are really very few people with whom you'd want to swap problems.

The major turning point for most people is to accept their insecurity and to stop trying to hide it.

It's a bright day when a person can understand that his imperfections are only human and that trying to conceal problems only makes them more obvious to others and even more difficult to correct. When energy is poured out to cover up faults, there's little left over to correct them. The point is to make use of your experience and allow it to highlight your shortcomings as well as strengths. That process defines you. Why waste time pointing out problems you can see in other people but are unwilling to look at in yourself?

Hurt demonstrates what is important to you more clearly than any other feeling. It does this especially in people who are vulnerable, who are most undefended against the hurt. You can't learn or grow from an experience you deny, including the experience of being hurt. Hurt by its nature is difficult to deny. Hurt, *hurts*. If you accept your vulnerability and regard it as proof that you're open and sensitive to your world, and accept that you are not perfect and stop trying to project an image of someone who is, you can profit a great deal from your experience of being hurt—see and understand yourself, including your shortcomings, more clearly, have the chance to overcome them and grow. If you need to pretend to others that you've already arrived, you are only setting yourself up for serious loss later on when you suffer the hurt of falling short of your pretenses.

Because our energy is limited, it's wasteful to use it in any way except in the pursuit of the truth, or to grow or to search for what's best in us. To do otherwise only drains, because we end up trying to justify what's simply not true. And when energy is enlisted to support a lie, it becomes increasingly difficult to tell what's real — we've invested so much of ourselves and our energy in what's false that to give up the lie seems like losing a part of ourselves. In time the fear of accepting the truth grows and forces us to deny more and more of what's real.

If the feeling that originally seeks expression is a painful one, instead of feeling a hurt or the anger over a hurt, the painful feeling is often buried and expressed in another way—as a symptom. For example, there are compulsive symptoms whose purpose it is to undo "bad" feelings or ward them off magically, as a ritual such as compulsive handwashing does. There are so-called conversion symptoms by which, instead of feeling, a part of the body is symbolically affected, like actually going blind instead of "looking at" painful feelings. There are emotionally aggravated physical illnesses, personality splitting, denial of reality. The list of possible symptoms is endless. The meaning of each is often highly personal and becomes clear only through uncovering the meaning of the feelings symbolically contained in it. Feelings may be blocked anywhere along the process— at the threat, at the hurt, at the anger, at the guilt or at the depression.

The point is that unless you decide that being

your best self is worth the pain and risk of experiencing the truth of your feelings, you are condemned to be led where your defenses lead you. What could you possibly learn about yourself that you don't already suspect? Do you think you are so terrible that discovering the truth would destroy you? People seldom fall apart when they finally learn the truth about themselves. The truth is usually that, like everyone else, they are flawed and they are not as good as they'd hoped, but still are better than they feared. Each of us is responsible for correcting those flaws that can be fixed and accepting those that can't so we can continue to grow and become what our potential suggests.

If you want to grow, begin by accepting the fact that like everyone else you are human, vulnerable, and subject to hurt—out of it can come your best chance for a liberating piece of the truth.

Some people don't pretend they're perfect but instead suggest the opposite, that they are the very worst of people, that they have no redeeming qualities and that their life is hopeless and useless. They have the same defensive problems, but don't know it, as those who claim perfection.

People who put themselves down and protest their inferiority are really saying, "Don't bother attacking me, I have already attacked myself and done a better, harsher job of it than anyone else possibly could." They deal with a potential hurt by trying to neutralize it in advance, by outdoing any potential critic. How, indeed, can they possibly be attacked when they themselves take care of the attacking? Much that they say about themselves may be true, but not nearly as true as they lead others to believe — they're just not quite as unredeemable as they claim to be. They also are trying to cover up. They do it by making their problems appear so overwhelming that it would seem hopeless to try to decide which problem is most important, let alone to change it. Why even bother? The end result of putting themselves down is precisely the same as for those who deny any problems at all. Both groups feel it's pointless to try to do anything about their problems. In the one case because they really don't have any. In the other because they have nothing but.

In the face of losses and hurts, it's remarkable how much alike we all are.

Many of us also set ourselves up to be hurt. Being hurt proves we're not at fault, or are helpless and therefore have no responsibility for our troubles. It also says someone *else* is the aggressor in our lives. Such people often use being hurt to control others by making them feel guilty. They can make your life miserable if you happen to become trapped in their web. They try to control and direct by creating situations where others are forced to do *something*! Once others do, they take it as outrageous hurt. The "injuring party" who has been caught in the trap now is made to feel guilty, which makes him angry at the person he's "hurt." His anger confuses him, makes him feel more guilty, because it's difficult for him to see the "victim" as the aggressor he really is. His guilt now keeps him in line, until the next time he is set up.

You can't win with such people. They frequently create a situation where to do nothing seems to be callously allowing them to destroy themselves. But if you respond to their helplessness, they only become hurt, claiming you are interfering, imposing your will or taking away their rights. And if you don't help it's taken as proof you didn't care. These people usually hold in their "outrage" until the moment has passed and wait for the most advantageous time to attack you for your negligent behavior. The best way to deal with such people is simply to point out that they indeed have set you up for the hurt, that you are angry at them for having manipulated you. Only don't wait as long as they did to bring it up. Tell them as soon as you're aware of your feelings. With feelings timing is very important.

The problems a person has in dealing with hurt are generally characteristic of his other problems in life. People who can't express hurt are often trapped in defensive patterns that control their reactions. Any hurt that's not expressed leaves some pain inside. Pain involves negative energy. When this pain is held in it depletes you of your positive energy, which is used to balance and contain it. Life seems less joyful. Thought and feeling aren't free. Concentration and productivity decrease. When pain from an injury is stored it continues to seek expression, but the defenses keep it from doing so directly. The lingering negative feelings may attach themselves to other negative feelings or may color your perception so that you find something to feel hurt about in nearly everything in the world around you. The withheld hurt asks to be felt everywhere. When you, for example, receive a gift, you may look on it as a bribe rather than a generous act. You're forever suspicious, sniffing out hidden ulterior motives where none exist.

The best way out of this situation is to try to identify the original source of hurt and to suffer and grieve for the original loss that caused it. Nothing resolves a loss better than feeling the appropriate grief over it. It's not easy to pinpoint losses if you're forever projecting rather than acknowledging hurt. In the case of another person behaving this way, the best you can do is to point out feelings that seem irrational, to try to encourage the person to stick to the facts.

People also feel hurt when they lose a friendship. A misunderstanding between friends can be one of the most painful and wrenching events in life. Friendships often break up because one friend betrayed the other's trust. Two friends share the same vulnerability. A friendship that's built on vulnerability in common can be close and beautiful. Both friends have similar weak points, and each tries to avoid hurting as he himself would not want to be hurt. Problems come up when one friend is unable to accept some hurt or loss and instead injures his friend in the same way, exactly as he was trusted not to. He betrays the friendship and, because he betrays a shared vulnerability, he also betrays himself. This kind of shared vulnerability demands nearly total honesty from both partners. The greatest hurt always has its roots in being dishonest in some way. This is the worst sort of pain, for in losing a friend this close, you feel as if you have lost a part of yourself.

The way to correct such a situation is to be entirely honest, allowing one friend to express the depth of his pain and the other to accept the blame for his callousness, thoughtlessness and cruelty. If a friend isn't willing to admit his role in causing pain the other friend has every right to avoid being close to him. Why should a person seek to be close to someone who has injured him deeply if that person isn't willing to concede his mistakes and role in the hurt? A person with so little insight and acknowledged responsibility for his actions isn't very trustworthy. If you allow him to become close again without a new and more honest level of understanding, you're only setting yourself up for another hurt. If you do that, it's time to ask yourself "why," because this time you're setting yourself up, asking for the hurt you already know is coming. It's foolish to continue such a painful friendship.

Of course, in a real friendship both friends understand that they will *occasionally* hurt and be hurt. They can accept this not as a weakness but as proof of their humanness. They don't see hurt as an excuse for discontinuing an honest friendship.

The losses most difficult to endure are those that can't be replaced but can only be accepted. The death of someone you love is shudderingly real, utterly final. The conciliatory words you wanted to say before can never be said now. The repairs you wanted to make in your love can never be accomplished. It is too late. The only changes that can take place now are within you, and your attitude.

Much of what happens in the process of grieving has to do with accepting the loss and coming to terms with one's anger over being abandoned and left alone. There's also frequently much guilt in being a survivor and in recalling old unresolved battles between you, the grieving person, and a loved one.

When people lose someone they love, they tend to play out all the patterns of defense available to them. Usually on hearing the news of the death of a loved one, the first response is denial. The bereaved often repeats "no, no, no" as if trying to deny the reality of the loss. Feelings of emptiness and isolation deepen. The grief-stricken person tries to control his feelings, to limit the loss and circumscribe the grief. He may wish he were crazy or act crazy to get relief from the pain. Symbolic offers are made mostly before, but also after the loss: "Take me instead," for example. Bargains are suggested and promises of reformation and purification are tendered. No use. The pain deepens and the mourner finds himself trying to pretend that this never happened, or believing in magic, following rituals blindly, doing anything to keep hope alive and pain away. But such pretenses are flimsy and the loss in all its sadness begins to be felt. Little by little the person's energy is drained, as a part of his world he once loved is taken away.

Each person must resolve his grief in his own way. Some losses are never settled, and a person learns to live with a sense of incompleteness and sadness. Usually the hurt over being left alone, and the anger over that hurt, gradually find some expression. Often it's against someone other than the person who has died, because getting angry at a dead loved one only increases feelings of guilt, which in the mourning process are very common. Usually when anger at the deceased can be justified, the guilt will pass. Sometimes when people who have lost someone important when they were children lose someone else later in life, their mourning process becomes extended. Such people seem to fall back on their childhood defenses, mostly denial, which doesn't work. Or they are re-immersed in the childhood loss as well as the loss in the present. Others spend their lives trying to work out their guilt by living a life of self-punishment. They need to try to direct their anger outward so they can be free. Grief that's inhibited eventually robs the mourner of his own life.

Again, to feel hurt is only proof of your vulnerability and humanness. Your hurt is a reaffirmation of your ability to form attachments, to become emotionally invested in the world and to find meaning in it.

A person who lives a life immune to hurt lives a life immune to joy. There is no way of avoiding pain if you wish to be open to pleasure.

When you feel hurt you need to ask yourself, "What have I lost?" Were you aware it was so important to you? If you weren't aware that what you lost was so important, why weren't you? Not to be aware of your emotional investments means you're dangerously vulnerable, unable to adjust and protect yourself as you should. Not all losses can or should be protected against, but you should at least know what's important to you. How else can you have an appropriate, realistic reaction to the loss of it?

It's also important to know how *you* experience hurt. Everyone has his own signals. Some people get a pain in the stomach. Others feel their hurt as pain in the chest. You can have a physical representation of any feeling. Tension and anxiety are frequently felt as muscles tightening in the neck, as well as in cramping elsewhere. Anger often brings on headaches. Guilt and depression favor the lower back. So when you look at any life situation and have feelings about it, note also your physical responses. In this way you'll become familiar with your reactions and will understand what your own physical symptoms mean. Often such physical expressions appear long before a person is aware of the feeling causing it, such as "butterflies" in the stomach before realizing you're anxious. You won't be able to use this physical information to your fullest advantage until you take an inventory of your own physical feelings and connect them to your own emotions. It may take some time to do this, but the shortcut this kind of knowledge provides is worth the effort.

Perhaps the truly most difficult loss of all to accept is the loss that forces you to see through yourself, to find yourself lacking in ways you were formerly unable to admit to anyone — most especially yourself. It also opens the way for the most important kind of growth toward reality.

At the risk of repetition, I should like to emphasize what I've said earlier in this chapter. What should you do when you have been hurt? If someone hurts your feelings, or causes you pain, express your hurt to that person as directly and honestly as possible. The simplest way is to say, "You hurt my feelings when you did thus and so." This approach may not always produce the response you want, but making the other person aware of your hurt is the best way to put your feelings back into balance. Being hurt drains your energy. Compensate for that drain by directing your negative feelings outside yourself, by unburdening yourself of the hurt or expressing your anger appropriately at its source.

Let your hurt become the other person's problem if he caused it. The other person may try to show you how you brought on the hurt yourself or how you set him up to hurt you or try to avoid accepting blame in other ways. Just be sure that you make your hurt known to the person who hurt you. This doesn't mean that you should ignore the other person's explanations, but don't let them get in the way of expressing your hurt and anger. Examine the other person's remarks for whatever truth you can find in them. Maybe you did set him up to hurt you. If you did, that's important to know.

The importance of being put in touch with the pain and pleasure in life, with your feelings and experience as they really are, is that it frees you to make the most realistic and positive adjustment to the world. Your feelings need to flow naturally. You need to settle problems as they occur, directly and honestly. If you can't learn something about yourself when you're hurt, you are missing an opportunity to grow or to change the way you deal with the world, as well as to check out the validity of your expectations. Expectations determine how each of us anticipates the world. And so our expectations are potential sources of hurt.

Expectations. A life which is full of them is usually full of disappointments. The lives that are the most desperate are the lives in which expectations are least real. To expect that other people will always be pleasant and will act in your best interests, even at the expense of their own, or to believe other people want to hear your sad story or enjoy your company when you are boring or draining, is another way of saying that you expect other people to take their cues in life from your hopes rather than from their own experience and feelings. Other people tend to look out for themselves. If you expect otherwise, you are being unrealistic and are needlessly setting yourself up to be hurt. Other people are not here to serve you or to make good on the losses and bad bargains you've suffered. Other people are here to find their way the best they can. Your unrealistic expectations of their behavior will make them feel used and treated as objects who have no feelings or rights of their own.

It comes down to this: It hurts to lose something important. It hurts worse to pretend otherwise. To expect more than reality can offer, only sets you up to be hurt badly, and needlessly.

CHAPTER THREE

Anxiety

ANXIETY IS the *fear* of being hurt or of losing something. Whether the fear is real or imagined, it *feels* the same. Anxiety varies from the mild apprehension of someone testing the temperature of the water before going swimming to the disorganizing panic of a person unable to control his bodily functions. Between these two extremes are feelings of being fearful, scared, edgy, jittery, concerned, worried, helpless, insecure, uptight, nervous, having cold feet, getting the shakes — all degrees of a feeling of uncertainty over one's personal safety.

Fear, like all feelings, serves an important purpose — in this case, to alert us to defend ourselves. So when people try to pretend they're not afraid, they seldom do themselves any good. Fear protects us, and we ignore it at our peril, whether out of a desire to appear strong or to evade the truth of our feelings. When fear warns us of danger, it's summarizing all the information being received by the five senses. Fear calls our attention to a possible threat to our well-being.

When you're exposed to a threat, your body responds by releasing powerful stimulating hormones into the bloodstream. These hormones make the heart beat more strongly and more rapidly and also direct blood flow to where it's needed most. In a time of stress the blood supply is usually diminished to the abdomen and the skin, and is increased to the muscles. Most of the physical symptoms of anxiety — cold feet, butterflies in the stomach, sweating, dilation of the pupils of the eyes and skin pallor — are caused by these hormones.

These stress hormones also make our minds "race," and increase our awareness of our surroundings. An excess of this puts us constantly on guard, which in turn tends to immobilize. Children living in cities under attack during wartime, for example, become so defensive in the face of chronic anxiety they seem to lose their personality. Most of us can't survive chronic anxiety without serious emotional consequences.

The intensity of anxiety often depends on the severity of the impending loss, the closeness of the threat, the importance of the loss to the individual and the strength of the person and his defenses.

What are most of us most anxious about? The answer generally is, losing our lives. Any psychology that doesn't consider the importance of the instinct to survive hasn't much to do with reality. Few of us actually observe the instinct for self-preservation operating in real life, but we can detect or at least respond to it fairly readily in the world of fantasy. For example, the great adventure story or film grips us and holds us in our seats as we identify with fictitious people threatened by powerful, seemingly invincible creatures, spirits, holocausts, earthquakes, sharks. The involvement these adventures arouse reflects our basic survival instinct. The feeling of taking a risk and surviving is invigorating. It gives a new sense of life. That surely is one reason why sports that involve risk are so stirring.

In the real world anxiety is common enough but the potential aggressors in our lives are seldom so clearly defined. They're more likely to be represented by the local bureaucracy that asks us to fill out a dozen meaningless forms during an emergency, wasting our time and causing us needless stress; or a government spending our money irresponsibly and threatening us with jail if we don't pay our taxes; or inflation or recession and their threat of unemployment. We often feel helpless confronting these threats. The aggressor is simply too powerful. Sometimes we're not even sure where the threat is coming from. The government, the economy are giant abstract threats, threats without faces or an approachable personality.

Moviemakers, novelists and television writers create adventures for us in which threats at least become identified as *real* characters who can be sought out, overcome or outlived. Our anxiety is stirred up, we see the enemy defeated and we feel a sense of release from our own unease. A sense of relief.

Most of us live lives in which much of the anxiety we experience is out of our control. We look for ways to express our instinct of survival, or end our feeling of helplessness. Our survival instinct is awakened not solely from an actual threat of death but also from a more general fear of dying. Most people fear the horrible finality that will dispatch them to nothingness, to nonbeing.

When confronting impending death, such as finding yourself in the path of a runaway automobile, the events of your life are often vividly recalled. This abrupt playback of past events comes from a sudden indiscriminate loosening of the defenses, allowing you to see the world within and the world outside more clearly, as they really are. Defenses are a delaying tactic. They slow reactions, protect you from potential emotional hurt.

There is a time for defenses and a time for survival. Fortunately, under great stress, the decision is out of our hands. The lifting of defenses becomes an instinctive act of survival. The mind is opened to seek out safety. This eleventh-hour opening of consciousness has also been seen in mental hospitals where, when faced with imminent death, some severely disturbed mute patients have occasionally begun to speak with feeling about their lives. It's as if the threat of death offered such great punishment that there was nothing left for these patients to repress, and so they could act without the restriction that shaped their behavior for so many years.

Most of us rarely feel threatened for our immediate physical survival. We have little sense of a real physical threat being overcome and the enjoyment of relief that brings. Our modern age probably has deprived us of something by removing us from direct personal contact with the elements of nature. We find ourselves in an artificial arena where our adversaries are arbitrary employers, demanding schedules, unfair practices and red tape—all of which create feelings of frustration and threaten us without giving us adequate opportunity for expressing our feelings about our condition. We live in an unfair emotional bondage. We've been coerced into selling out our instinct for personal survival for something called "long term security," without being told beforehand of the consequences. We never imagined that in our day-to-day living and working experience we'd be most threatened by our protectors. Worse, we seem to have few resources left to combat such threats, because to fight the system seems overwhelming. Don Quixote may have known what he was doing when he chose windmills as adversaries.

If we were to examine the "system," we'd see that the security it offers is elusive. It depends on the system working. When hard times come the system isn't working and the loyalty of the company toward its employees may be difficult to discern, and the situation may produce more anxiety than security. The modern world is driving many of us crazy.

The answer is that each of us — to whatever extent possible — must take our survival back into our own hands. We may not do as well financially, but if we can lower the anxiety level by being more in control of our own destiny, we've come out ahead.

When it seems impossible to manage directly the stress of working for a corporation or contending with government bureaucracy, other outlets for resolving tension have got to be found. One such is a sport that offers physical and emotional challenge that can be met and overcome. It's very rewarding to pit oneself against a mountain in winter and conquer the steepest slopes. You may not have beaten the boss, you certainly have not made the tax laws any more equitable, but you have overcome a real challenge, and you have demonstrated your ability to "make it." The system may no longer work, but you still do!

It's our modern civilization itself that's at the root of a great deal of our anxiety and stress. Industrialization has often progressed at the expense of the individual. The exigencies of corporate and industrial life dictate that we suppress our instinct for survival and suffer in silence the anxieties such a life produces—a depleting experience, because to suppress any emotion requires energy. To live in a world where some company professes to know what's best for us and expects us to go along blindly with its policies is putting the survival of that company above our own. No company or organization that places the survival of itself over the well-being of any single member can ever act in keeping with the real needs of the individual. We sense this and feel uncomfortable on the job, a little used, perhaps, a little like an impersonal number. Many businesses today are creating products on one end of the assembly line and dehumanized workers on the other. Working with faceless machines in which one's only interest is in keeping one's hands or clothing out of the gears is *boring*. The usual way people defend themselves against such monotony is to block it out and retreat into the world within. This turning away from the world only adds to the feeling of boredom. Anxiety and boredom tend to go hand in hand, and often result in such disorders as depression and alcoholism.

This sense of helplessness in a mechanized world gradually undermines our ability to take charge of our private lives. We tend to erect such a protective screen against our anxiety at work that when we return home those same screens stay with us. When we look for the nurturing and love that we're missing on the job, we're often disappointed as we frequently make unrealistic demands on those we love to compensate us for our unhappiness. Often our stressful anxiety makes it difficult for us to see that those we turn to at home also have their own needs. As work stress increases so does the imperviousness of our defenses, and the richness of our personal and family life diminishes. Often we don't recognize what's really happened until the damage has already been done. The intimacy of the family unit is undermined. The husband feels unfulfilled, the wife feels martyred, the children rebel. We tolerate such situations because we don't recognize or admit the problem. We "reason" that the times aren't the best, that one should be thankful for bread on the table. But what job is truly worth this kind of emotional suicide? It is little better — sometimes worse—than nothing.

We can only react purposefully to a threat if we perceive it. Few of us are so self-aware that we're able to understand exactly what we fear, and therefore we're unable to relieve fully our feeling of anxiety. Some are even unaware that what they are feeling *is* anxiety.

Just what does it feel like to be anxious? First, you feel uncertain, agitated, or unsettled. There's a growing sense that something bad is about to happen, a vague sense of impending loss. Events seem to be out of your control and working to your disadvantage.

How do you cope with these feelings? Before you can do anything about your anxiety, you must first be able to admit that you are anxious. This may not be as simple as it sounds. Many people have peculiar notions about their feelings. They believe to admit feeling frightened is to admit being weak. They deny their anxiety and try to pretend nothing's wrong. Whenever you deny your anxiety you only undermine your ability to defend yourself from whatever is threatening. To say that you're not anxious is the same as saying there's no threat. How then do you explain your feelings? And what purpose do they serve?

When you feel anxious you're perceiving a threat even though you may not be aware of it. Don't ignore anxiety. It means that something you consider important is being threatened.

When a person has a severe perceptual problem, he often distorts the reality he confronts. The world of a deaf or blind person differs greatly from the world of the rest of us. Yet the world of a blind or deaf person differs less from that of a sighted person or one who hears, than it does from a person who is so rigid in his defense that he alters reality. A blind person lacks only sight, not perspective. A deaf person lacks sound, not understanding. Such people have their own ways of perceiving reality. Handicapped people have less room to operate, less margin for error than others. Their alertness and ease in responding to a warning feeling such as anxiety is a measure of this. They pay greater attention to their working senses and consequent feelings, and as a result are often more aware of the world around them than the rest of us.

Lighting a match in the same room as a blind person frequently makes him agitated and he immediately seeks out the source of the smoke. This increased alertness to smell is a compensation for his loss of sight. It's not only that the handicapped person is more acute in his remaining senses; the rest of us have had our senses so bombarded by our environment that we tend to block out the incoming stimuli that would alert us to what's threatening.

Each of us needs to raise his awareness of his own feelings and perceptions. This doesn't mean that like the blind person we must investigate every puff of smoke, but certainly we ought to be aware that the smoke is there so that we can be ready to react as necessary. If we try to block out what makes us anxious, what frightens us, we set ourselves up for greater suffering. Better to do something about problems when they're small and can most easily be coped with. If we constantly block a threat from our awareness it consumes more and more energy. As it grows it eventually does break through and overwhelm us.

When a defense stands between you and your ability to perceive your true feelings, it also stands between you and your best chance of survival. To be anxious is to feel uncomfortable. It's *supposed* to feel uncomfortable. If anxiety weren't uncomfortable, people wouldn't do anything to get rid of it. The feeling of anxiety is best removed by removing the threat that caused it, not by defensively denying or ignoring it.

If you're in danger you should know it. If you rely on someone else to act in your best interests when you're threatened, then something is very wrong in your life. To place responsibility for your safety in another person or in an institution may be helpful in quieting your fears for the moment, but eventually it undermines the natural process of self-survival.

Being anxious and afraid may tend to bring back childish feelings of helplessness, but admitting you're afraid doesn't mean that you're a child. When we feel afraid it's only natural to wish that someone "bigger," more capable and powerful, will come to our rescue. Such fond childhood hopes tend to wither naturally in the shadow of adult experience. We see more clearly every day— if we're looking — that the only person we really can count on for help is ourselves.

Modern society sends us two conflicting messages: be self-reliant, be yourself, take charge of your own destiny; conform, play the game, be a "good" citizen. Individuality is often labeled eccentricity, tolerated in theory only; conformity is expected in practice.

Meeting our obligations to society and earning its prescribed rewards too often may not fulfill our emotional needs. We want something more but don't know where to look. What we find is a sea of anxiety. Out of fear, we tend to follow a course chosen by others who claim to know the "right" direction. No wonder so many of us feel anxious so much of the time. We're beginning to lose our initiative, our sense of ourselves, of our own life's goal and purpose.

For many these words may sound inconsistent with the hard cold practical facts of life. A person has to work, to get along or worry about being fired. Well, yes and no. That's the message we've been conditioned to accept. It isn't necessarily the reality of our best interest or even survival. It's the message of somebody else, of a structure that has its own self-interest, not necessarily the same or even consistent with the individual's in question. A fact of life is that many of us give up or give in too easily, without even looking for alternatives or testing them. We fear the uncertainty of newness. This does not mean that we should give up job, family and society for some mystical inner voice. But at least give your best self a chance. Listen to yourself, accept your responsibility for solving the threats to your life and well-being, at least to the extent that you can from the resources within you. This at least is a start at being a free person. And isn't that what we're all supposed to be about?

Aside from the anxiety created simply by our society, each person needs to come to terms with the threats and fears of his own inner personal life — based on the prejudices of his upbringing (a prejudice is an organized set of feelings that can be triggered by some external stimulus). Whether the object of the prejudice is a group, an idea or an attitude, a prejudice is only altered by experience.

As children we learn our prejudices out of fear. What begins as a fear of a specific object, situation, or person tends to become generalized. A fear of a dark place, for example, becomes fear of the dark. Our prejudices are like reservoirs of bad feelings and get in the way of our finding the truth. We fear the stranger only partly because he may cause us harm, but more because he is not party to *our* particular perception of the truth. What he says about us derives from what *he* perceives about us. We tend to fear the stranger because he can see our imperfections, because he may hurt us by uncovering the truth about ourselves.

Each of us feels vulnerable in a different way. If you know your vulnerability you know a great deal about yourself. As we've seen, everyone is vulnerable to the loss of a loved one, the loss of control, and the loss of self-esteem. Each of these types of loss creates a corresponding category of anxiety. Some people are so sensitized by their particular life experience that one of these categories takes precedence over others and colors the way they see the world.

Dependent people are especially vulnerable to loss of love, either because as children they experienced such a loss or because they lived with the threat of separation or rejection. They go through life feeling a loss even before they have lost anything. They may even precipitate a potential loss just to get their anxiety over with. They often create a feeling of helplessness in other people, who feel angry at them for making them feel that way and reject them — and so another loss. Because dependent people tend to act in a regressive and infantile way when threatened, little they do seems effective in preventing the losses they fear. Their unwillingness to assume responsibility for their life only adds to their grief and further alienates the very people whose love and affection they fear losing.

Dependent people see the world in terms of loss or rejection and are likely to find evidence everywhere they look that such a loss is imminent. Take this case, for example, of a woman who was so wounded by losses and separations as a child that she saw the losses woven into the fabric of her life more clearly than she saw her life itself. One afternoon when storming out of her daughter-in-law's house after an argument, *she* began to feel abandoned by the act of *her* own leaving. She drove along the superhighway following another car. After a few miles she began to feel a peculiar attachment to it. In her mind the other automobile was showing her the way home. It was taking care of her. The farther away from her daughter-in-law's home she drove, the more old feelings of abandonment as a child returned. After a while the car she was following turned off the highway and she was left in tears, feeling abandoned by the world and unable, literally and figuratively, to find her own way home.

This woman's experience is typical of the ways incidents in our present can trigger the unsettled sorrows of our past, making the world a screen on which we project our hurts.

The next kind of loss that produces anxiety is the loss of control. Whether it's power, money, position, influence or title that we value most, few of us look as unhappy or as desperate as "controlling" people who feel they're about to lose control.

People who most fear losing control are those who make a special point of being in control all the time. They live by rules. They feel most comfortable when they know the precise limits of a given situation. They can relax only when they're sure they understand how everything fits. Even then they may be on the lookout for things that *could* go wrong and they invent extra routines to perform to make certain that what hasn't gone wrong won't. When things do start to get out of control they tend to get more and more involved in the rules and details of the system and begin to regard them with an air of permanency or even religiousness. They imbue them with a ritualistic or magical quality in an effort to exorcise their anxiety. Consider a lady or gentleman who makes a revision of the shopping list by rows to correspond with the supermarket displays, who keeps the house pristine, who pays bills by return mail, whose checkbook balances to the penny, whose calendar is planned months ahead, thereby getting the unknown under control as well. Is this person really in control?

In fact, for many controlling people, their order and routine seem more important than their feelings. Because the loss of control is so frightening, they try to control the pieces of their world in increasingly minute detail, making still longer and more accurate lists, keeping a still neater house or office. They would do better to admit they feel hurt and anxious and to realize that this is what makes them feel out of control. When you experience a feeling without hiding it, it passes most quickly and drains you the least.

The loss of esteem also triggers anxiety. It may appear as a fear of failure, a fear of being exposed as worthless or a fear of being ridiculed. People who live in fear of being embarrassed often try to hide their real feelings. They may pretend that their feelings are unimportant, or that the test of their worth didn't count, as for example the student who goes through school barely passing because he's afraid of taking the risk of trying and not being the best; he can always tell himself, "If I'd really studied I could have been first in the class." He may even believe it.

Such people are often competitive and unsure of their worth at the same time. They feel anxious not only when they're put down, but when other people exceed them. They rarely act as themselves, but in a way they think will make them appear worthwhile to others. They rarely make an honest effort to succeed, but just enough to give the impression of success. Ironically, the effort needed to succeed is usually only a little more than that required to save face.

True success can't be achieved until you're willing to be judged on your performance. Not wanting to be so judged, a person overly concerned with esteem shies away from making a full effort in order to protect his fragile self-image. He really isn't sure he *could* be first, and not knowing how well he could do, he dreads ever finding out.

All these three issues of anxiety-producing loss reflect growth stages everybody has lived through. To the extent that these issues of the past continue unresolved in us, we remain vulnerable to similar situations in the present. And to some degree all three issues—losing love, control, or esteem—are capable of triggering feelings of anxiety in each of us.

Now the question is: how do we go about

managing anxiety? Since anxiety is a warning, it's vital that we first understand what dangers we're being alerted to — the warning must be broken down into usable information.

Sometimes it's awfully difficult to tell if the danger causing the alarm is in the present or in the past. The lady who became attached to the car she was following simply couldn't make that distinction. When she was a young child her mother had gone off with another man. She couldn't face the loss and chose to deny it. She acted as if it hadn't happened; to others she seemed hardly to miss her mother. The price she paid was to live a life where anything that might remind her of losing her mother re-created the original feelings of loss. By avoiding the grief of the original loss, each new loss, large or small, symbolically triggered the old one.

In managing her anxiety that came from a loss presumably too terrible to acknowledge and face, this woman was encouraged to take stock of her strong points. She re-examined her life and saw how capable she was in so many areas of managing on her own. She came to understand that the impact of the original loss depended for its power on her helplessness as a child. In time she began to reconstruct her self-image. Seen from this new perspective, her life suggested that she might now be able to bear the childhood loss of her mother. She allowed herself to grieve, mourning what could not be retrieved, accepting what was beyond her control. In the process her feelings were liberated, made available to be invested in the present. All this did take time, and the woman is still quite sensitive to loss. She always will be. But at least she's no longer a captive of her anxiety. She no longer sets up her losses in advance. She's able to enjoy life because it's no longer automatically tainted by the past.

Managing anxiety primarily in the present is less difficult. When you feel anxious for reasons not clear to you or when a situation that should make you happy only makes you feel threatened, stop and think. The first step in getting control over anxious situations is to ask yourself, "What is it I'm so afraid of losing?" Asking that question sometimes gives enough distance to begin to solve the problem. The question begins to define the answer. The office worker afraid to ask for the raise, the tenant afraid to arouse the ire of his neighbor whose radio blasts him deaf every night, the boy afraid to ask the girl for a date—and vice versa in these changing times!—all may feel generally anxious without knowing why until they begin to stop and think and ask themselves the question: "What am I afraid of losing?" And in reply may come, respectively, the answers: my job, a "friendship," my masculinity, my femininity.

Most people face some anxiety every day of their lives. Lawyers become anxious when they have to appear in court. Accountants become anxious before an audit. Professors become tense when they have to lecture. Students become worried before exams. Hostesses become jittery before a party. Directors become distraught before opening night. Theirs is preparation anxiety. It's the fear of being a flop, of losing face. This anxiety, in moderate amounts, helps to get a person charged up to do his best. It's common to everyone who stands up to be counted. But often the level of anxiety associated with performing is so high that it keeps many even from trying. Moderate so-called stage fright, however, is not a disease and only when it actually prevents you from working does it need to be treated.

Some people, though, live their lives as if they were giving one continuous performance after another every hour of the day. They fear they're being judged by everyone who sees them. Because they've not accepted themselves they worry no one else could either. They're afraid of being confirmed as worthless. They live from one unsatisfying event to another, wondering who'll find them out next.

Chronic anxiety is difficult to manage and painful to endure. A person suffering from it feels constantly as if he were about to suffer a great loss. He uses up most of his energy trying to hold his anxiety in check. As a result even small amounts of stress quickly overwhelm his ability to cope. As his defenses become spread over too wide an area in an attempt to cover all possible threats his anxiety begins to leak out everywhere. Defenses become useless. In fact, he becomes so caught up in the management of his defenses that he has little energy left over to live.

Managing such severe anxiety may require professional help, including an anti-anxiety medication so that a person is able to regain some of the energy used by his defenses and apply it to solving his problems. It's difficult for therapy to have much success until anxiety is reduced to manageable levels. There's nothing like feeling better to feel better. Chronic anxiety is aggravated by the stresses of day-to-day living: traffic, shopping, the media, the demands of a family, personal relationships, not to mention the economy, the unsure prospect for the world, shortages, aging and disease.

Many people suffer from anxiety without realizing it because their defenses against anxiety keep them from being aware of themselves. The defensiveness of the average New Yorker is a good example. They have to shut out a lot each day just to get breakfast down. Our society makes emotional cripples out of many people who can't cope with the lack of clear-cut goals and rewards that have little real meaning. We still need *some* space, time, privacy and peace, if only for a few minutes each day. We need an opportunity to get in contact with ourselves, to listen to our thoughts, to pay attention to our feelings.

Even though it seems impossible at times, the best way to manage anxiety is to avoid unnecessarily threatening situations and to begin to make yourself the most complete and strongest person you can be. To do this you need to accept who you are, take responsibility for your life, and make certain that you are heading in the direction that is right for *you*. This is a difficult job. To be one's own person, you need not be entirely free of anxiety, but at least you can know what you fear and be free to change what threatens you.

A free person accepts responsibility for both the good and the bad in his life. He is aware of his own vulnerability and instead of concealing it he uses it. He allows himself to be open to the pain of his world. Through that special window he can see more clearly, because he feels more. A free person doesn't waste time and energy getting involved in things that can't be changed but instead focuses on the areas he can affect. He doesn't let the world "get to him." He simply defines what his goals are and works honestly and energetically toward them.

One of the most important goals of life is to become familiar with yourself in a positive way. To reach this point requires acceptance of your limitations. You need to understand that no matter how badly you may have been treated or what your personal circumstances happen to be, no matter how cruelly abandoned or rejected you may have been or where you are in life now, you are always in charge of your own life — you have the primary responsibility to make good on your talents and abilities. Hopefully the disappointments and rejections you experience will someday be seen as a proving ground for you.

If you're a person who's been brought up in a dependent way, your outlook need not always be one of disappointment and hurt over losses. Your own special sensibilities about being dependent may allow you to become a person with extraordinary nurturing qualities that allow you to identify with and help people who haven't yet outgrown their dependent ties. Once a person has overcome his own dependency problems he becomes free to give, to support, to encourage and to sustain—to do everything that's the opposite of draining other people. The anxiety he felt in being afraid of dependent losses will gradually disappear as he begins to see himself as a person of strength.

In the same manner controlling people, once they learn to overcome their defensiveness, also have a great deal to give. They have a special understanding of loneliness and isolation. People who've learned to overcome their need to be in control all the time can be very helpful to others in showing them how to organize and reach toward a self-fulfilling goal.

And people who've been anxious about self-esteem can learn to be less self-centered and more concerned with the job they're doing than the impression they make on others. They can learn to respect what they do for itself rather than constantly worry about being worthy in the eyes of others.

So when weaknesses are converted into strengths, people are transformed from dependent, controlling or esteem-seeking members of society to nurturers, managers and performers, and each has a great deal to give and teach the others.

Although anxiety carries the threat of impending loss and injury, it doesn't obscure the very positive and real aspects of its other function—to alert and build up the self into its highest potential. We can do this by accepting the hurts that have come to each of us, having done with the pain, learning the lessons of our early experiences, and growing into the best person we can salvage from our past and create through the actions of our present.

Each of us is the architect of his own future, and if we use our best personal building materials we have nothing to fear. Merely being on the road to the discovery of one's best self lowers anxiety. The rest is work and time. Everyone moves at his own pace and in his own way.

No one can create your life for you. No one is supposed to. Others may point the way, help define your goals, but the work, the burden, the responsibility—and therefore the joy—are yours alone.

CHAPTER FOUR

Anger

ANGER IS the feeling of being irritated, miffed, teed-off, irked, annoyed, furious, enraged, "burned."

People get angry when they have been hurt, and so everyone has angry feelings from time to time. When a person tells you he never gets angry, he's really telling you he doesn't recognize his anger or is concealing it because he's afraid of what it may reveal about him.

You don't have to be seething with rage to qualify as being angry. Indeed, most of the anger that people feel is not violent or difficult to control. It is irritation or annoyance, the usual response to everyday disappointments. Anger, like anxiety, is just a category for a wide range of feelings, all of which have in common the fact that they are reactions to hurt or loss.

How does anger result from being hurt? Any emotional injury drains your energy by creating a negative feeling that has to be resolved in some way. The natural reaction is to redirect that negative feeling outside you, at whatever caused the pain. This is the most effective way of settling anger, but it's not quite as simple as it seems, because the cause of the hurt is not always clearly identifiable. Here's an example that illustrates this —the anger of a grief reaction:

A ten-year-old boy's dog is killed by an automobile. The boy feels great loss. The dog has been his constant companion. The boy can't believe his dog is really dead. It hurts too much even to cry over his pet—the pain of the loss is so great the youngster can't express any of it directly. He's not able to work in school or concentrate on anything important. He sits in his room and stares at the television set without enjoying it. All his energy seems to have been used up trying to contain the hurt. A part of himself that he's identified with his dog no longer exists, and he dearly misses that part. He's angry that the dog has died. But *who* should he be angry at for the death of his dog?

After a few weeks the boy begins to speak with anger about the driver of the car—he should have been more careful, he was driving too fast — and once even accuses the driver of trying to hit the dog. He begins to dream he saw the car that killed his dog crashing into a wall. After a while he remembers that his dog always chased cars and he wasn't able to break him of the habit. He feels angry at himself for failing as a trainer, and irritated with his parents for not offering to help train the dog. Later he begins to direct his feelings against his dog for not knowing any better than to chase cars. Gradually the boy's anger is released and his energy for other activities slowly returns. He's able to concentrate in school again and get back to living his life as usual.

Expressing anger over the hurt that causes it allows an emotional wound to close. In this case the youngster naturally began to seek out objects he could get angry at: first, the driver of the automobile, then the automobile, and then even a little at himself — much of that anger had the quality of, "if only I'd acted right I wouldn't have lost my dog." Next, he shifted the blame from himself to his parents, and finally, much diluted by time, the anger was directed at the dog. Having vented his anger at all possible targets, he finally came to the right one—the poor dog itself—and his wound was allowed to heal.

If any loss is to heal in the best and most complete way, the anger it generates needs to be allowed full freedom of expression. The first step in repairing an injury is to make the hurt known by getting angry. The second is to direct that anger toward an appropriate target. Expressing anger is a natural, healthy response and is necessary to keep one's emotions in balance.

This isn't to say that anger is a pleasant feeling. There's a great deal of stress involved as one's blood pressure climbs and heart rate accelerates.

But if the angry person can release the emotional and physical tension that has built up inside, he will eventually feel better. Trouble comes when the true source of the hurt is unavailable to get angry at or when doing so causes so much unacceptable pain the anger is blocked and the angry feelings fester inside.

Some people feel that it's wrong to be angry and refuse to admit to even the mildest annoyance. Others dislike getting angry because it's unpleasant. Some people mistakenly believe it will just go away if they ignore it, or are afraid that if they get angry they'll lose control, create a scene, embarrass themselves or hurt others. Whatever the reasons people give for not getting angry they are self-deceiving. You can never justify burying your anger.

To hold anger back only adds to the hurt that caused it. The defenses that prevent the anger from flowing naturally outward now channel it inward, directing it against you. Someone always pays for anger. Far better it be the one who caused the pain than the one who received it. When you hold anger in, you only punish yourself.

How much anger needs to be expressed to balance a hurt? It varies from person to person. Some can merely mention their hurt to the person who caused it and their anger is over and done with. Others have so much pent-up anger that they go into a rage at getting a wrong number. Of course it's never possible to have a perfect balance be-

tween anger and hurt. That would mean one particular loss could be cancelled by one particular
feeling. No matter how angry the young boy got
over his dog's death, for example, his hurt could
never be completely erased. No amount of anger
could bring his dog back. But showing no anger
over the loss would have been the same as denying
it happened—and in the same process denying his
feelings. Allowing the anger to flow cleanses the
emotional wound and initiates healing.

Some people fear admitting hurt because they
don't want to appear weak. Ironically their unac-
cepted hurt and unexpressed anger over it undermine them and only make them feel less strong,
less able to admit future hurt, setting up a vicious
cycle that eventually shuts out reality.

Although showing anger is necessary to balance a hurt, it's sometimes difficult to know what's
"appropriate." For example, how do you express
anger appropriately at a loved one who has just
died from a long and painful illness? Is it appropriate to complain to the heavens for making the
loved one of such fragile substance? Is it appropriate to curse the deceased for his physical shortcomings or his neglect in not seeing his doctors
sooner? Such angry feelings even if justified are
difficult to admit when the person who caused
them is dead. You feel guilty getting angry at
someone who's already paid the greatest price.
Nonetheless we often *are* angry at the loved one

who has died and left us, however irrational or inappropriate it may be. Then how do we express our anger over such a loss?

A recently widowed elderly woman was looking for help for her unrelenting grief. When she talked about her late husband she complained that her eyes burned. Her husband had been a rather meek and simple man who, although he'd done his best, had just managed to provide her with the basic necessities. She would clench her fists when talking about her exasperation in trying to manage a small apartment in a deteriorating housing project. To be angry at her late husband would only have made her sadness greater by increasing her guilt. Because she did love him and his memory was one of the few things he left her that she valued, getting angry at him was too great a risk. So, safe targets for her anger were chosen from the many government agencies and other people she encountered in her daily life. She got angry at the Veterans Administration for not sending enough money, at the secretary in the health clinic for not being courteous, and at her children for not being attentive. Perhaps these attacks weren't always justified, but in time her anger at her husband for dying was dispersed among several people, none of whom seemed to notice the extra anger coming their way, and in this way her grief began to lighten.

This process of releasing anger by directing it outward in an appropriate way is central to the whole issue of hurt and anger. If anger isn't expressed but is defensively held inside, it begins to destroy the person it lives in, eroding everything that feels good in that person. Yet some people seem to be angry all the time and are *still* irritable and edgy. Why aren't they well-balanced and happy? After all, they're always letting their angry feelings out. Or are they? Just because a person acts angry doesn't mean that he is settling a hurt in a way that allows him to come to grips with it.

Chronically angry people often feel short-changed in life and blame others for their problems. They seldom receive what they think they deserve. They don't realize that few people in life get much of anything without working for it. But to admit this would require that the person accept some of the blame for his own failure. Usually this is too frightening because it opens the floodgates: "If I'm at fault for some of my failures, *maybe* I'm at fault for all of them." This is too depressing and overwhelming to contemplate; more comfortable to guard against any attempt at self-blame by continually directing anger outward — an anger that becomes a defense and indeed a way of life. Any passing slight adds to the reservoir of pain. Anger is continually discharged — scatter-shot — without ever coming to grips with the original source of the hurt. Confusion, frustration and escalating bitterness result — searching for a target that can't or doesn't want to be located.

The direct *appropriate* expression of anger, on the other hand, is a necessary part of a healthy emotional life. Don't regret having angry feelings. Everyone gets angry when they get hurt. The only people who don't get hurt and therefore angry are those who claim to have no vulnerabilities. And people with no vulnerabilities have no sensitivity. They also can't respond to another's feelings or share, or be intimate, because they have no access to their own feelings.

Sometimes when a hurt is relatively slight a person may bury it rather than express it in anger. This can become a bad habit, because many small silent hurts can add up to produce a big anger. When that happens no single cause of the pain seems important enough to justify getting as angry as the person now feels. To let out that much anger at any of the little wounds would seem inappropriate, so it's held in. Which is the way to disaster.

When angry feelings are allowed to flow naturally to wherever they appropriately lead, what happens? The answer is different for everyone, because everyone has his own style and personality, and so each hurt feels different accordingly. But basically, once the matter is confronted openly, and honestly, the anger, once out, is out. The slate is clear again! Difficulties occur when people try to modify their natural feelings to make them more acceptable to others. In so doing they vent only part of the anger and still feel trapped. Nothing adds to a person's sense of frustration as much as trapped anger.

The person who truly understands his feelings

doesn't sit and brood in silence over pain, constructing angry fantasies of retaliation. Instead he openly confronts the person who hurt him and as quickly as possible tells him exactly what he thinks of the situation with as little fanfare or exaggeration as possible. He does *not* rub the other person's nose in his misdeed, for example, nor does he play the role of the injured party who now has a right not merely to retaliate, but also to humiliate.

People who act out their fantasies of revenge don't merely want to get even, but to destroy. Admitting that you feel this angry is a good first step toward finding the proper perspective. Many people are reluctant to get angry because their fantasies are so violent they frighten and confuse them. They worry they'd really go overboard if they let loose and prove to the world that *they* are the monsters. They don't realize that their fantasies are the result of the holding back itself. So they do nothing. Both these alternatives, overreacting and not reacting at all, are unhealthy.

There are better ways of releasing anger. Here are some points to remember: When someone has hurt you tell them so directly and openly . . . "You hurt me" . . . and also tell them exactly why. Do this in private. Don't unnecessarily set them on the defensive. It will only make them feel like retaliating rather than listening. Be firm as you need to be to get your point across but try not to be punitive.

If the person denies he hurt you, point out the facts again and say you know what you feel. If the other person tells you you are too sensitive, that he was just kidding, point out that people vary in their sensitivity — one man's kidding is another man's pain. Tell him you want to make him aware of your sensitivities so that he can take them into consideration in the future. If you feel the other person hurt you on purpose, say so. When people hurt others intentionally they often do so out of anger. If this is the case, ask that he be more direct in expressing his anger next time, telling you the problem without causing you unnecessary hurt. When someone hurts you like this, it's up to you to act in control, the other person is already acting childish. Retaliating seldom solves the problem and often obscures the point that both parties are trying to make. It causes guilt, pushes people apart and wastes time and energy.

Expressing anger properly is healthy and restoring, but there are many people who can't seem to handle anger at all. Feeling angry makes them feel badly about themselves, and so they keep their feelings bottled up. People fear getting angry for different reasons, depending, to some degree, on their background and past experiences. Let's go back to the three personality types — dependent people, controlling people, and esteem-seeking people.

Dependent people are afraid that being angry

will prove they are unlovable. They're afraid that expressing their anger will turn away the people they need for nurturing and support. Many of these people had difficulty in being nurtured as children, and grew up with a feeling of insecurity over their own worth as a person. Such people have learned to swallow most of their anger and often feel trapped, helpless and empty. When they do get angry they're often inappropriate in their choice of target and out of control. Their rage may be directed at a "safe" target, such as a helpless child — just like themselves. Many child beaters are in this category. People who felt unloved in childhood almost never feel comfortable getting angry at someone they love. Instead they may act helpless or beaten as a way of getting to others. It's as if they were saying, "See, look what you're making me do to myself." Their approach almost never works — they only succeed in pushing the people they need farther away from them.

Dependent people go through life struggling angrily and half-heartedly for their independence. They may feel someone is holding them back, not giving them what they're entitled to. Their anger is very much like a child's who feels mistreated and wants to get even but doesn't know how. Because their goals tend to be so dependent on others, they don't make an effort for themselves where it counts. Their anger is turned in on themselves, and their energy is quickly dissipated.

As for the controlling people, they tend to equate showing anger with losing control. They try to ward off hurts and anger by elaborate mental manipulations. But feelings simply can't be as controlled as they'd like. Feelings want to be expressed. Trying to control them merely reshapes the way they may appear but it doesn't change the feeling itself or diminish its impact. People who are especially interested in control seem always to be looking for excuses for their feelings. They intellectualize, rationalize, project, isolate and otherwise confuse the real issues. They hardly ever see anything in a simple or uncomplicated way. For a controlling person to say, "You hurt me and I am angry with you," is very difficult. To be vulnerable, for them, is to be out of control.

Anger is a powerful feeling, and to channel it away from emotional expression by intellectual means requires much energy-consuming fantasy and thought. These in turn remove you so far from actual events and feelings that you often forget what the hurt was about. The first step in settling anger, the admission of the hurt, becomes the first stumbling block that controlling people need to overcome. It's doubly hard for them because, although they can easily talk about their feelings in words, the words don't translate into emotions.

Not only do they have a difficult time expressing anger, they also find it exceedingly painful to accept proper responsibility for hurting another person. If you get angry at a controlling person for hurting you, you may find it an especially unrewarding experience. When you make your point the controlling person will probably give you a detailed explanation to prove his actions were out of the best intentions. The fault is *yours*. The hurt inflicted on you wasn't really a hurt at all, but your own shortcoming finally brought to life by his generous behavior that, of course, was for your own good. Confused? You're supposed to be.

Controlling people can be difficult to deal with because they are simply so intellectually involved and so far removed from their feelings that they aren't really honest. Worse than that, they have a limited ability to accept their dishonesty and so give defensive excuses when cornered. They see themselves as people who must be perfect and use their formidable defenses to lure you away from any meaningful discussion of their feelings, their anger, or *their* weak points.

When these people *do* show anger, it's extraordinarily unpleasant. One has the feeling of being in the same room with a mad tyrant. They're unable to say simply, "You hurt me." Their anger is so tied up in intellectualized defenses that it's never really free to be expressed simply and directly. Instead, they lash out in torrents of rage. Such people need to learn to express their anger a little at a time and, most of all, come to realize that they can be angry without losing control—without going to pieces.

People most worried about esteem and superficial appearances often suppress their anger by hiding behind an act of some kind. By exaggerating their reactions they deny their real feelings. For example, they may act wildly, hysterically angry, but when asked about it won't admit anything is really wrong. "I was only pretending," they will say. Such people would rather play the role of an angry person than admit to their real feelings of anger. To reveal their own feelings forthrightly is to risk being judged. Instead of risking the loss of your respect or admiration, they disguise their anger. Their feelings often manifest themselves as physical complaints. Everyone is familiar, for example, with headaches caused by held-in anger—"I've got one of my 'sick headaches,'" goes the refrain, instead of, "I'd like to kick your teeth in," which may be closer to the anger felt. By masking real feelings these physical symptoms spare the person from being judged and rejected for being angry (and hence being "bad").

Another way these people handle anger is to "split off" any angry outburst from themselves as if it didn't belong to them at all. Later they may conveniently forget the outburst and refuse to accept the anger as their own. The problem with managing anger this way is that it uses up so much energy, wears you out, and the anger is never really directed at those who caused it. The people who are to blame aren't even put on notice that they've been hurtful. The injured person hasn't directly defended or expressed himself, and so there's no relief from the cycle of hurt and anger.

These three personality types as they relate to the feeling of anger have been discussed in some detail because each of us is our own unique mixture of all three. Everyone shares some defenses in common with all three types, but in widely varying degree.

Some of us have large reservoirs of anger that require all our energy to handle. Such a backlog of unresolved feelings needs to be decreased to levels where we begin to have energy available for investing in the world outside. It's difficult to react to the world in a fairly easy, outgoing manner if you continually feel anxious that you're going to lose control and blow up.

When you're filled with negative feelings, you may be ready to do battle at the drop of a hat, not to mention a word or a look. Some days are like that for everyone, of course. There are days when something goes wrong that's hard to identify, and so we go through the day being irritable and snippy, looking for people to get into arguments with and being generally unpleasant. But to live one's whole life this way is intolerable.

In the traditional forms of psychotherapy, people with such long-standing painful feelings are led back into their pasts to uncover the source of the original pain and then come to terms with it. The theory is that the person, now older and wiser and having the perspective of many years' growth and much suffering, will be able to view the old pain with a new distance and accuracy and so be better able to put away his old defensive devices for dealing with that pain. This method doesn't always work so simply and neatly in practice. Just to grow up is to gain a new perspective on past hurts, successes, loves and hates so we can see the present more in keeping with what *is* and less with what *was*.

The best way to change one's perspective on the past is to deal honestly with the feelings of the present and to resolve those feelings as completely as possible as they occur. If you're angry, show it. Don't take refuge in a headache. Don't pretend you're above such feelings. And don't try to ignore them and bury them in the past.

Every therapeutic process takes place in the present, whether or not the events being discussed are from the present or the past. What you should ultimately learn in any form of therapy is a better way of discharging feelings so that the minimal residue remains from emotional encounters and you are free to interact without emotional legacies.

The way to change your attitude toward the past is to become as honest as possible in the present. Being totally honest is the best way to live in any case. Existing at levels of lesser honesty takes up too much energy and always relies on defenses. You can't live your best life telling lies—

especially to yourself. Becoming totally honest is the first step to becoming free. Expressing your feelings openly is the second.

Other people may feel you're overdoing it the first time you express strong feelings such as anger openly. Just remember that most people avoid making any kind of disturbance — "don't make waves," we're told — and your anger, even if it's mild, will appear unusual. Some people will be startled or upset by your honesty. That's too bad. You just try to speak out with the truth as you see it. Most people worth getting angry at—people you care about — will accept or at least tolerate your new attitude. Those who won't don't respect your right to be a person.

It may take some months for you to feel natural expressing your feelings, especially anger. When you first begin to be open, you may feel your emotions build and rush to the surface, almost sweeping you away with them. It's tempting to close down and rein them in again. Be brave. Don't hold back. Let them out. The process of learning to express feelings is painful. It requires your determination. Stick with it. It will pay off as trapped feelings of hurt and anger from the past come out and escape piggyback on their counterpart feelings of the present.

Now you'll no longer feel as if you must always be on guard to hold back forbidden feelings. As you become more accustomed to being open, you'll be amazed at how little time and energy it takes to keep current with your feelings. Saying "You hurt me" will literally become a matter of course. People who are dishonest will find it more difficult to deal with you and will keep their distance—for which you can be grateful. Life will be fuller and richer because there will be more of you available for the people and things you love in the present.

In time something else important will happen: the feelings you now hold in aren't your feelings from the long-forgotten past of early childhood, but the feelings of present, everyday life. The angers of this week, yesterday, this morning are now the culprits. Not large hurts, but little events insult and hurt you every day. It's your faulty pattern of dealing with feelings on a day-to-day basis that causes most of the difficulty in your life and it can be recognized and adjusted without hauling out all the heavy baggage of the past. The process of growth and becoming is continuous. If we're open to it, it can offer new opportunities to find ourselves and reshape the course of our lives. Just as adolescence offers new opportunities to re-examine the issues of independence, control, esteem and identity, the remaining years of our lives present chances to redefine ourselves, to seek our freedom and learn to be ourselves without apology.

Again, the secret to success in this continuum of growth is to be honest with your feelings at all times. Every time you're dishonest you create a problem, reinforce a negative energy or bolster an old defensive system which then distorts reality and interferes with your ability to cope with the world.

If you're hurt and don't experience the expected anger, ask yourself why not. Where has the anger gone? Are you hiding it? Are you pretending it doesn't bother you? Why shouldn't you feel angry when you're hurt? Are you afraid of appearing vulnerable in front of a particular person? When you're afraid of opening up in front of a particular person, but have been able to do so with others, it may mean you don't really trust that person. You're afraid that exposing yourself to him would be a risk. He might hurt you further or retaliate. Tell him that! If your natural expression of a feeling is blocked by the presence of another person, that person is keeping you from being honest and free. The inhibitions you feel may actually be *his* defenses, working to shut you off. Pointing out how his presence inhibits you and makes it difficult for you to be your best and most honest self is your best weapon and most valuable insight. Avoiding people who enhance or encourage your dishonesty is probably a good idea. It's hard enough being honest without inviting situations that bring out the worst in you.

Of course, there are times when expressing anger creates problems. Everyone is familiar with the demanding and unappreciative employer who treats employees like objects, making them feel insignificant, constantly hurting them and using his authority to intimidate them. The employees feel irritable and defensive and tend to perceive the boss negatively even when he has no negative intention. Expressing anger in a situation like this carries its complications, not the least of which is losing your job. If you have an employer like this you have a choice — you can learn to accept his negative ways without becoming personally involved, or you can change jobs.

But of course that's not always as easy as it sounds. Many people feel trapped in a job out of fear of change or because they don't want to lose their seniority. The protective structure provided by seniority and unions is remarkably analogous to our psychological defensive systems. Originally they were constructed to keep us from being vulnerable and to protect us from possible hurt. Then we became dependent on them and found it hard to function without them. We have a way of recreating in our immediate environment the same problems and patterns that imprison us in our own minds.

I agree it's true that the way our present society is constructed, even when we become free of our own defenses, our openness tends to bring us into some conflict with the defenses and controlling patterns of the world we're trying to survive in. Still, there's always room for increasing the openness and access to your own feelings and to the feelings of others. That's the real world, the one most accessible, most rewarding and over which you can assert the maximum healthy control for your own good.

Often the people we become angry at are people without faces or names, people who pass by so quickly we hardly notice them — the bus driver who slams the door in our face, the police officer with a chip on his shoulder, the nasty waitress, the irritable ticket taker, the obnoxious cab driver, the authoritative lawyer, the pompous physician. All hurt us in ways that make us angry, but we need the services and assistance of these people and are forced to endure their negative manner and hostile attitudes.

But how to deal with anger created by people like this? The physician will often become defensive and arrogant when confronted. The lawyer will find some way of getting back at you that you will undoubtedly pay dearly for. In the best of worlds it should be possible simply to tell the person he has hurt you. But many of these people don't really care. What then? To take affront at these episodes and make them a personal issue is the worst thing you can do. You'll end up wasting a great deal of energy and gain very little. Still, even in these situations the moment may come when you can usefully give your opinion of their behavior straightforwardly and honestly. Tell the cab driver when you pay him that you felt he was rude and therefore you're not tipping him. Tell the person who's surly to you, "You have a chip on your shoulder, and I'm not going to knock it off."

Again, the important thing is to let it be *their* problem, not yours. Be thankful that your own feelings are settled in ways that leave you human. Aren't you glad you aren't the bus driver, being so angry all the time? If someone willfully hurts you, it's their problem, but to let them gain control over your feelings and make you angry for the entire day, that's your problem. The best way of dealing with such people is to be in tune with your own feelings—if you are, these people can't easily push you over into an angry mood.

If your anger starts to build up, here are some ways of letting it out. Imagine the person who has offended you dressed in ridiculous disguises, such as red tights and feathers. Or imagine him at a state banquet, nude and eating with his fingers. A ridiculous fantasy helps dissipate anger nicely and will put a smile on your face that will drive the other person absolutely crazy. Besides, the other person is already wearing a ridiculous disguise by being an angry person. Your fantasy will help you put that into perspective.

There are other ways of letting anger out. Write a furious letter, but don't mail it. Keep it and reread it in a month. You can telephone the offending person, keeping the button down, and let all your anger out. Anything that will put you in imaginary contact and release your feelings will work very nicely. Even if you feel silly, try it. You'll be amazed at how much better you feel. Pounding a pillow for ten minutes also provides tremendous release for some people. So does screaming. But be careful, these devices can become ends in themselves and should only be used as a substitute for the real thing when the actual person is unavailable or you haven't yet worked up the courage and ability to confront him directly.

Also take time to recognize the physical ways *you* feel anger. Everyone has a special different place for feeling anger. Some people get a tight feeling in the neck, others get a burning sensation. Think about where *you* feel anger and take notice of it. It's your signal to do something to let that anger out.

Letting anger out as you feel it makes *all* the difference in the world.

CHAPTER FIVE
Guilt

GUILT IS the feeling of being unworthy, bad, evil, remorseful, self-blaming, self-hating.

Guilt is the result of holding anger in so long that it turns against you. Guilt is a complicated feeling, and just as people are hurt by different acts, they also feel guilty in different ways.

People who feel guilty punish other people by their presence alone. They tend to reinforce the negative side of the world and ignore the positive. They are joyless. They don't feel worthy to accept what others give and so they don't feel fulfilled themselves and can't give back. Although guilty people may not be able to feel or admit to their anger, there is an angry quality to their outlook that makes other people feel rejected and drained. They seem to wallow in their negative feelings as a way of punishing themselves. Since most of us feel guilty about something in our lives, the guilt-ridden person also reminds us of unpleasant feelings we'd prefer to forget. Guilty people invite rejection and hurt by refusing offers of help and

99

friendship. It's as if they feel better when other people treat them badly.

Like the angry person, the person who suffers from guilt has a hard time directing his feelings toward the source of his long held-in anger. He lashes out indiscriminately, and finds himself in a position difficult to defend. Imagine how foolish, unlovable and unworthy such a person feels when he kicks the family cat, screams at his children or slams the door on a total stranger to relieve his frustrations. The resulting guilt comes not only from realizing that his reaction has been inappropriate, but also unnecessarily hurtful. He feels as cruel as the person who originally injured him. He begins to doubt his worth and to turn his anger inward, reinforcing his feelings of guilt.

As we've seen in the previous chapter, when anger is held inside, it festers and expands until it becomes a person's entire inner world. Unexpressed, it often takes the form of angry fantasies and dreams. Almost everyone has experienced this. Someone hurts you and circumstances — or your own reluctance — prevent you from telling him. You feel used and taken advantage of. In your mind's eye you see your tormentor and seethe with anger. While walking down the street you become so absorbed in your anger and in imaginary ways of getting even that you take the wrong turn. You begin to relive the scenes of your injury, and in your imagination you retaliate with a vengeance.

Perhaps you humiliate your victim in the presence of others and embarrass him by cruelly pointing out his faults. Or you imagine yourself making a phone call to a powerful friend whom you instruct to fire the person, or to dress him down for injuring you . . . you who are such an important friend of his powerful employer. Or it's early morning. Your tormentor is tied to a post. He refuses the blindfold. Good, you'll watch him eye-to-eye. You give the command to the firing squad: ready, aim . . . Revenge!!!

If angry fantasies are allowed to grow as the hurt and its anger are kept in, they can lead to feelings of guilt. Soon you, who normally picture yourself as calm and reasonable, find yourself entertaining fantasies of physical violence and excruciating torture. The medieval grand inquisitors had nothing on you. Your imagination, prompted by the trapped anger, rivals the worst monster of the Late Late Show. Worse yet, you catch yourself smiling in the mirror. You're even enjoying it! What do you do in the face of this sinister revelation about yourself? Feel ashamed, become unglued, or just feel exhausted by it all? You might begin by realizing that the hurt just possibly wasn't intentional to begin with and you're making the situation worse than it really is. Sometimes this understanding is enough at least to begin to relieve the anger, release you from the preoccupation, and save you the guilt.

Sometimes it's not. The angry fantasies and the guilt they create may continue to feed on themselves. You may even forget the original hurt that started all this, and become preoccupied and unable to stop thinking about revenge. You also realize *you* are the one having these bad thoughts. The other fellow merely hurt you, but you're living in a hate world. You feel worse. Now you begin to suspect there's something wrong with *you*. Maybe you really deserved to be treated the way the other person treated you. Maybe he saw the evil potential in you that you've so nicely demonstrated to yourself. You begin to feel so badly about yourself that thinking about the original hurt actually makes you feel better. A guilty person like you deserved what he got, right?

Guilt like this can get a grip on a person and begin to direct energies inward as it begins to punish, often in illogical, uncontrolled ways. Memory selects only negative recollections. Evidence of former accomplishments and good deeds that would support a positive image are more difficult to find. We're so convinced we must be bad that we struggle even harder to cover our anger—after all, we have no right to it. We become more closed, less communicative, more uncomfortable to be around—with so much energy going inward, we only drain those around us.

So, severe guilt becomes a terrible trap. If the guilty person begins to express anger, he may feel he's only proving he's the evil person he secretly suspects he is. Guilty people often fear punishment for their anger, which they secretly believe they deserve. They may even act in a way that invites rejection or hurt because they actually feel relieved when they're punished. They seem addicted to unfulfilling jobs and punishing life situations. It's no wonder. The constant external torment at least spares them the burden of self-punishment. It is a tortured way to live.

The way out of such guilt isn't easy. You need to look at the reasons you weren't able to express your anger in the first place. What were you afraid of? Were you unaware you were being hurt? Did you fear rejection by the person who hurt you? How did you get trapped into holding your anger inside? What did you fear would happen if you let it out? You need to understand something about what got you into trouble before you can go back and try to resolve it. The anger you convey has to be justified by the actual hurt itself—by reality, not by your fantasies. Misdirected anger, unfounded anger make you feel rotten and solve nothing—in fact make you feel worse.

The most difficult kind of guilt to resolve is the guilt that's created not by a single incident but by a number of incidents over a long period of time. We become rigid in our pattern of behavior, hold back all hurts and deny all anger. We go through life guilt-ridden, blaming ourselves for everything that goes wrong.

It's especially guilt-producing to be angry at

someone you feel you're supposed to love. Children and parents, for example.

An anxious mother or father may have mixed feelings about their child, might even occasionally *secretly* wish to be free of the responsibility of parenthood, of adulthood in general. But such parents often can't accept these "awful" feelings, instead feel guilty and direct their anger inward. To be angry at one's children, many of us have been taught, means to be a bad parent. And to be so angry that sometimes we wish they weren't there ... well, *that's* a capital offense. But the thought isn't father to the act, and it's *acts,* not thoughts or feelings that are subject to outside rational punishment.

Actually we all feel angry at our children from time to time. Trouble comes when we're angry at our children and try to pretend we're not. That often makes for insincere compensatory displays of affection—born less from real affection than out of guilt. The children feel there's something wrong but are confused and naturally reluctant to show *their* true feelings. We parents have disguised our anger so well in our giving and our children are so hungry for it that they feel it's wrong even to think their wonderful parents are insincere. Their needs cause them to distort their perception. They need loving parents so they perceive their parents as loving ... *almost.* They're also pretty smart. All this makes for unhealthy orientation to the world for a young child who begins to let his needs shape his reality. And the overdose of giving makes growing up harder for the parent, who may now feel committed to supporting his image as a giving parent and so gives to support his own disguise, not because he feels it and wants to. This parent may see the child as a stumbling block to his or her own growth and development. The real stumbling block, though, is the parent. Afraid to grow, he or she uses the child as an excuse, but covers it up. We should be in the business of *un*covering.

Parents like this often undermine any uncovering of anger by the children, especially at the parents. If your child says, "I hate you," as children frequently do even over trivial matters, and if you're insecure about your own anger toward the child, you may say, "Don't *ever* say a thing like that. How dare you . . . you hurt my *feelings* . . ." The child feels guilty and learns that letting out anger is bad, especially at parents. It's also unsafe —he may lose his parent's love. Better to shut up, like the bad little boy or girl he or she must be. And the very angry adult he or she is likely to become if this exchange becomes a pattern between parent and child.

Now take it from the other viewpoint—feeling guilty and angry at your parents. We like to think of our parents as all-giving people who will always take us in and accept us. Unfortunately our expectations of how our parents are or should be aren't always borne out by reality. Parents are simply people who happen to have children. Because they happen to have children doesn't automatically make them more responsible or even loving. It offers an opportunity and a challenge, but it doesn't necessarily build character. In fact for some people parenthood erodes what limited emotional reserves they have. Not *everyone* should be a parent, and not everyone who is a parent can be a good one.

The resentment between reluctant parents and their children feeds on each other's disowned anger. Often the product of such a parent becomes an adult who can't deal with his anger. He harbors resentment at his parents, whom he sees as artificial and phony, *acting* in a giving manner but withholding what the person most needs — love and support. The anger that couldn't be voiced in childhood still seeks expression, and the scene is set for an emerging adult who feels guilty for continuing to harbor anger and resentment. He may even be afraid of doing anything that is strictly for himself, because he feels that in fulfilling his own desires and needs he's in some way voicing anti-parent feelings — which recall his old anger and evoke buried guilt.

Breaking out of a pattern like this is difficult, but not nearly as difficult as continuing to live a guilt-ridden life. If you're forced to live in constant fear of hurting your parents' feelings, your life becomes a painful replay of your confused childhood. But confronting your parents face-to-face does run the risk of producing more bad feelings than it resolves, unless now as an adult you have dropped your defensive attitude and approach the problem in a calm, straightforward manner (not a confrontation nose-to-nose like little kids but a direct and honest exchange like adults). Be forewarned, though: parents who produce guilt in their children have a way of acting helpless and hurt when they get older. They can express such a sense of loneliness and isolation that the guilt aroused by a head-on confrontation can be overpowering for *you*.

The best policy is to stop pretending to your parents that you don't feel what you do feel or that your feelings don't matter. If your parents have upset you or made you feel guilty simply point it out. If you tell your parents and all they can do is tell you how much you hurt them by telling them that, there's practically nothing you can do about *that*. Nobody's listening to you. If that's the case, if there's not even a willingness — or ability — to listen, then you've little to draw on—except your own capacity for self-punishment if you endlessly persist. What should you do to please such a parent? You'd better go about your business of living the best life you can and hope but not expect your parents will be happy for you. These are the terms to think in, if you're to break loose from the emotional chains that have kept you bound in guilt.

Guilt-producing people, such as some parents, are always best dealt with by being perfectly honest and straightforward — though not by being provocative, as if restaging *Who's Afraid of Virginia Woolf?* Here's an example: a telephone conversation between a woman and her manipulative, guilt-producing mother. It's intended to illustrate that honesty helps to take away the burden of expressing anger and puts the problem back on the parent, where in this case it belongs.

Mother: You never called me back.

Daughter: I've been very busy. Bobby has a cold, Charlie's getting ready to deliver his talk at the California sales meeting and he's been pretty tense.

Mother: Well, I decided that it would be a good idea to go to Los Angeles with the two of you. I could come out after the meeting and we could spend the next two weeks together.

The daughter, who has not included her mother in her vacation plans, is thinking of a dozen different ways to say this. She considers saying: "Look, mother, we haven't made any definite plans yet and besides it may not be possible to get reservations." But she knows mother might question why and her flimsy excuses would instantly be suspect. She'd be accused of not wanting her mother around, not loving her. She'd then have to overreact to prove to her mother that she really still loved her and make an offer to get together with her if chances permitted. Of course her mother would then investigate the reservation situation in Los Angeles like a travel agent and call back within the hour to announce that she'd found reservations for the three of them. You cannot mess around with a mother like this! They act helpless to arouse pity, but become as inventive as one of Agatha Christie's sleuths if they suspect you're avoiding them. Our daughter tries a direct, truthful approach.

Daughter: Charlie has told me he'd really prefer to be alone with me on our vacation after the meeting, that he works very hard and doesn't want anyone else around but me. That means no children, no mother-in-law, no work.

Mother: Oh. [The truth has stopped her in her tracks for the moment.] But I was planning on it. Besides I won't be any trouble. Your sister and brother-in-law invited me along on their vacation.

Daughter [being straightforward-honest and also suspecting her sister is still quite sane and wouldn't do something like that]: Then why don't you go with them?

Mother: Well, it's not settled yet. Besides, I told them I'd probably be going with you and Charles. But if you don't want me to go . . .

Daughter: Well, you shouldn't have spoken before you knew our plans. . . .

It was important for the daughter not to wander from the truth. By telling the truth she forced her mother to react to the actual situation rather than to any possible defenses the daughter may have had. She didn't try to avoid her mother. "Avoiding" is an old game and her mother knew it well. The mother's only power over her daughter lay in the possibility of making the daughter lie, catching her at it, and then in a show of hurt, create guilt in her daughter. By telling the truth, the daughter was dealing from her greatest strength. If she'd fudged on that, said something she hoped would be more acceptable to her mother, she'd have trapped herself in her mother's game-playing. She told the truth. If her mother couldn't stand the truth, it wasn't the daughter's fault—the guilt was off her shoulders. She would have to learn to accept her mother's feelings of rejection as the creation of her mother's personality and lifestyle and not feel guilty over them.

Remember, you owe no one the obligation to lie. You always owe yourself the truth.

Your parents' expectations for you can also lead to guilt. Their plans for you may reflect *their* own unfulfilled goals rather than *your* potential or gifts. As a result you're encouraged to measure yourself against a standard your parents themselves couldn't meet. So you're placed in the tough position of having to please your parents before pleasing yourself. If you're a child of such parents you may achieve great success in their eyes and still feel miserable about yourself because you don't know what success is in your own right. If you live for your parents, who will live for you — *your* children? Thereby forms a vicious circle. It's hard enough to try to do your best at a difficult task without having to feel you're letting your parents down by pursuing — and achieving — your own goals.

Remember, in the end only you can know what's best for you. When you don't act as you really believe and feel, you can't function at your highest level. To go against what you believe just to please someone else always turns out badly anyway. You can never adequately defend a cause or goal you don't believe in.

There are subtle parental pressures that can bind you long after you've grown up and should know better. It makes you feel very guilty to become angry at parents who have made great personal sacrifices to send you to school or help you toward a career, even if they were also actually trying to live their life through you. However subtly hinted, parents' martyrdom doesn't go unnoticed. You feel obligated to make good your parents' sacrifices ... "*My* parents shall not have struggled and sacrificed in vain," say you, the noble, self-sacrificing, *guilty*-feeling child.

There's another unhappy consequence even if you manage to fulfill the dreams of your parents, feeling uncomfortable all the way. At least, you may figure, you've not hurt them by going along— they'll now be proud and pleased that you are a doctor, dentist, pharmacist, plumber, garment worker, teacher, whatever. Not necessarily so: You may have done *so* well that your success is seen by your parent not as a fulfillment of his dreams but as a put-down of him. "My son, the doctor," can carry mixed emotions on the parent's part—envy mixed with pride. To succeed in pleasing can be to succeed in displeasing as well. How do you feel then? How can you win in a situation like that? You can't. You can mostly feel anger, pain and guilt. It's better to try being yourself.

It's true, of course, and it's natural that when we're young we look for acceptance and understanding from our parents and tend to trust their advice and guidance above all others'. And chances are your parents had the best of intentions about you, just as they did about themselves. But they're only people, only human, some wise, some not so wise. All tend to have the same problems and blind spots where their children are concerned, whatever the varying degree. All sincerely believe they have only their children's best interests at heart, but that does not make it so and it can make for an enormous burden on the child. Torn between finding himself and pleasing his parents, he has insufficient emotional support to pursue his own interests and insufficient talent to succeed in the areas his parents do encourage. He may never have the experience of performing at his best. Instead he feels defeated or worthless. Worst of all, he may feel unable to justify pursuing what he loves. By not developing what abilities he may have, he even begins to doubt these. He's unhappy, feels incompetent. He's also angry at his parents—whether he admits it or not—and if not, eventually feels guilt over his anger.

To get out of a bind like this you've got to learn to believe in your feelings and accept yourself as you are. If your parents haven't yet accepted themselves, how can they ever accept you anyway? If they need to prove that they could have succeeded had circumstances only been different, then they need you to live that missed chance for them — which, of course, won't work for them or you. In any case, the purpose of your life isn't to justify theirs. Becoming acceptable to yourself is enough of a responsibility, and it should be your first priority. What is your life worth if it's ruled by anything other than the search for the truth about yourself?

Obviously, though, somewhere along the way it's not unlikely your parents will be hurt. But the truth is that their deep-down hurt is not so much over you as it is over their failure to fulfill themselves. That realization often is a long time in coming. But by allowing yourself to support their unrealistic expectations of the world you have only at best delayed it and prolonged their unhappiness. It's foolish to lead your life to protect your parents from looking honestly at theirs. Maybe they don't want to, or can't. That's understandable. It's also true, nonetheless, that accepting each other as you are is the best and only realistic way. You will probably have to take the initiative. It's risky, it hurts, and you can be hurt. If you try it with them, approach with caution. But don't hold back living your own life.

If you're afraid that acting in your own best interests will hurt others, that fear can inhibit you from acting at all. It's natural to feel anxious about risking the love of other people by acting in a way you're honestly convinced is in your best interests. There needn't always be a good-for-you, bad-for-them equation, but it's often the case — at least from the other person's viewpoint—and it can be a considerable bind for you if you allow it to overwhelm you.

Such binds can be excruciatingly painful for young children. Consider, for example, the child who continually is told by his parents something to the effect of . . . "If you're good you'll act the way we want you to, and of course you're good because we wouldn't love you if you weren't . . ." Instead of learning to judge right from wrong on the basis of his feelings and experience this unfortunate child is encouraged to suspend his feelings and judgment and accept his parents' without question.

Trouble comes when he wants to do something his parents won't approve of. If he goes ahead, he worries he may lose his parents' love. If he suppresses his own desires he undermines his ability to grow from his feelings and experiences. He gets caught in a bind and becomes confused and ambivalent about taking any action at all.

To resolve ambivalent feelings, nothing is as helpful as a strong sense of one's self. Such a self-view doesn't form overnight, and no one's self-view is fixed. Everyone has the capacity for growth and for redefining himself by an honest encounter with reality. If you don't avoid ambivalent issues but meet them directly and try to solve them, they will become fewer and fewer.

The questions on which most ambivalence is based are universal: Am I good or bad? Weak or strong? Smart or stupid? Independent or dependent? Free or controlled? If you're uncertain about the answers to these questions, you'll feel ambivalent whenever they confront you. Because people are afraid that in facing the truth about themselves they may find themselves lacking, they tend to avoid such basic either-or questions. Facing them is the first and often most important step in solving them; and *accepting* the answers, however difficult, is the best way to decrease the unease of ambivalence.

What is it you want for yourself in this life? What are you doing to get it? What is in your way?

Who put it there? Why have you waited for a crisis to force you to act? These are the larger questions that follow the first ones. Again, by facing them you begin to help free yourself from the paralysis of ambivalence. The questions beg for the answer —decide who you are, what is best for you.

There is, of course, an important balance to be found between allowing others to run your life and acting without concern for anyone but yourself. This chapter is not an invitation to do whatever you want to avoid guilt. The modifying considerations, as always, involve treating others with mutuality and compassion, learning to love and respect yourself and your potential, nurturing yourself as a precious gift, and treating other people in the same way. Don't allow other people to use you or coerce you into denying your feelings out of fear of hurting them. But be certain you don't run over them in the process. Your freedom from guilt doesn't depend on abusing others.

The most common sort of guilt comes from realizing you've done something truly hurtful to another person. To deny responsibility for that hurt only reinforces your sense of guilt. The best way to relieve yourself of such guilt is to accept the blame for your actions, to apologize and to repair the damage you've done. This has a remarkable way of easing inner tension and making all parties feel better.

All of us feel guilty at times. Our guilt becomes a problem only when we don't understand it. We've seen that most guilt results from anger that hasn't been sufficiently expressed. If you feel guilty, find out where your anger is coming from. Understand how you were hurt. Make appropriate amends if you've hurt someone (*appropriate*, not endless *mea culpas;* let the amends fit the "crime"). If you feel guilty because you've let someone down, reconsider according to whose best interest you were acting in and by whose lights you let someone down. At least *look* at the situation—just possibly you may not have been entirely at fault. Possibly you've not been at fault at all.

People who make you feel guilty often use being hurt as a weapon. Producing guilt in others is a powerful and cruel device; it causes feelings to go underground, clouds up the issues that caused the original anger. It's very difficult to settle conflicts with another person when you're led to argue from your weakest, most defensive position. When someone plays on your guilt they draw out a less mature, more defensive person from inside you. The guilt brings out the childish part of you, the person who is most afraid of being punished and most fears being unlovable. It is also the part of you that eventually— if the person keeps it up— may be tempted to strike back in kind, which then evokes the same response in the other person: You hurt me, I hurt you ... Eventually both of you become guilt-ridden, and no anger gets resolved.

The only thing to do in a situation like this is to be clear about your feelings and to state them clearly. Point out that you believe the other person is using his guilt to hurt you and that no matter how much hurt you might have caused it does not justify retaliation by overkill in a guilt-producing way. One of you has to take the responsibility for setting limits. The person who is healthier, who has the best understanding of his feelings, should say "enough is enough," and stop. It takes two to argue. Hopefully that healthier party will be you.

Even so, after all the good and right and healthy things are said and done, most of us will continue to feel some guilt when we get angry at those we feel we're supposed to love. I hope it's clear by now that we've got to express our anger and hurt regardless of who hurt us. The proper expression of hurt redirects negative feelings outside of ourselves and is vital to restoring our emotional balance. It's true that expressing your anger may sometimes be perceived as hurtful by others, but you can't afford to take on their burdens, not at the expense of your own life.

Your ultimate goal in life is to become your best self. Your immediate goal is to get on the path that will lead you there. Why should you feel guilty if you refuse to be intimidated by a person who persists in standing in the way of your being that best self or who is "hurt" when you finally manage it? You'll never really please (only ap-

pease) such a person—even if you diminish yourself forever. If your healthy growth is viewed as a
hurt by someone—that will have to be their problem.

The highest love a person can have for you is
to wish for you to evolve into the best person you
can be. No one owns you, no matter what your
relationship. You are not here on this earth to
fulfill the unmet dreams of a frustrated parent or to
protect another person from facing the reality of
himself or the world. You are here to develop and
grow, to do your share to make the outside world a
better place to live, to make the immediate world
you live in, the world that is you, as honest and as
true to your feelings as you possibly can. Of course
compromises must be made with resources of
money and time, but hopefully your life goal won't
substantially change or be deviated from. If that
happens, your life, no matter how hard you try,
will only be an excuse for the truth of what you
are, your contribution to your loved ones will be
limited by that lack of truth, and you will be on the
embittering road to deep anger and its partner in
the killing of your dream—guilt.

It needn't happen. Don't let it. I hope something of what you find in these pages will be of
help to you in seeing that it doesn't.

CHAPTER SIX

Depression

DEPRESSION IS the feeling of being "blue," unhappy, melancholy, "down in the dumps."

Like guilt, depression occurs when anger is trapped and turned inward. In this case, the anger becomes hatred and begins to rob life of its meaning. It takes energy to make one's world a livable place, and the depressed person has little energy to invest. Obviously when a depressed person and a happy person look at the same autumn landscape they are reacting to the same external world. Assuming that their senses are intact, the sensory impressions they receive are largely the same. Yet there is a great difference in the world each finally experiences. The happy person looks at the landscape and sees in it a reflection of his good feelings. The depressed person finds only additional reasons for being depressed as he calls to mind people now absent, his inner emptiness, his worthlessness, and worst of all, the contrast between his inner sadness and the brilliant world around him.

Our moods color our world and shape our reality.

In depression, energy seems turned against the self. Rather than allow his feelings to flow naturally, the depressed person regards each angry feeling as proof of his worthlessness and recoils from expressing any anger. Even so, he often appears angry as his overwhelmed defenses let bits of anger leak out here and there.

Although depressed people often feel sad, depression differs from sadness. Sadness is the feeling of depletion that follows a hurt or a loss. When people feel sad and ask themselves, "What have I lost?" or "How have I been hurt?" they can usually come up with an answer that makes sense. They can express their anger over their hurt and pain from their loss. Their anger hasn't been buried, and if the hurt is set straight, their sadness usually disappears.

When people are sad for a long time, without understanding what their sadness means, they often lose touch with the event that caused the sadness. Depression is the result. Their sadness just stays there, fed by a deep reservoir of anger and hatred. They feel worthless. Depressed people are always struggling to hold back their anger, and this very act of holding back depletes them further and can make them feel sick. Even though sadness and depression may sometimes feel the same at a given moment, they are not. The sadness of everyday life dissipates. The sadness in depression, on the other hand, is trapped. Left alone, it grows.

Ordinary sadness passes with changes in fortune. Depression does not. Sadness is a passing phase in the natural flow of feelings. Depression is a disruption of the flow of feelings.

To understand a particular depression you need to know the real feelings involved. Does the sadness seem reasonable compared to what's been lost, or is it blown out of proportion? If the depressive feelings fit the loss, you can often set yourself straight by identifying the loss, releasing the anger, and making appropriate amends when necessary.

This is straight-forward depression, the kind that responds well to talking out with friends or simply sitting down and quietly putting your feelings together with the events that caused them.

Unfortunately most depression isn't so clear cut. Pointing out the events that caused the original hurt is seldom enough to reverse a severe depression. When you turn anger against yourself, self-hatred builds out of proportion to reality, causing you to be defensively secretive. (Such guardedness isn't always totally bad — it's a sign that a person at least recognizes that there's something wrong and may be able to take steps to correct it. Such depressed people often appear to improve in silence. In concealing their thoughts from you they also guard the progress of their recovery; their defensiveness often makes them inaccessible to words.)

Severely depressed people can sometimes be

reached by working with their guilt feelings, since guilt is often the most accessible of their feelings. In a hospital experiment, a number of depressed patients were sent to occupational therapy eight hours a day, five days a week. Each patient was given a large bowl containing several thousand tiny colored beads, some smaller bowls and a pair of tweezers. The patients were instructed to sort the beads by color and place them in the smaller bowls. It was extremely tedious and could not be completed in a single day. At the end of each day, however, the occupational therapist would examine each patient's work, dump the carefully sorted beads back into the larger bowl, and tell the patient to come back and tackle the job again the next day.

Since these patients were not communicative and couldn't be reached by the usual methods of psychotherapy, nothing about the patients' problems was ever discussed. Nonetheless they showed a marked improvement. The method apparently worked because in some way these patients felt they were being punished for their "wrongdoing" and were being allowed to make restitution for their "evil ways." They were given an opportunity to work off their feelings of guilt by turning their anger *away* from themselves and directing it at a safe target. In the process their depression gradually lifted.

The need for punishment in depression — at

least the chance to undo the harm that some depressed people believe they've done to others — seems an important part of the cure. Often when severely depressed patients start to get better they voluntarily take on such menial jobs as scrubbing latrines and floors. This sort of behavior — in or out of a hospital—seems to provide a working combination of self-punishment and directing anger and energy in an acceptable way outward—both at the same time.

In fact, directing energy outward is the first step in breaking the self-perpetuating cycle of depression. A person who feels depressed may have little inclination to get out and just do something. It takes an enormous amount of energy to be depressed. The best start may be solitary activities such as drawing, sewing, gardening, do-it-yourself repairing, cleaning cellars and attics and closets. All these offer a channel outside oneself without the pressure of socializing. Sometimes reconstructing a diary is helpful to sort out the events that have led to the present difficulty. Also helpful is to make a schedule of daily activities and trying to stick with it so that each day has a chance to provide something positive and rewarding. You don't have to be on top of the world to manage routine chores, and they may help you get off the bottom.

Everyone has had feelings of sadness, and most of us have felt depressed at one time or another in our lives. To be depressed is to feel lifeless, inhibited and drained. Bodily functions are slowed down. Depressed people frequently develop constipation and have sleep disturbances. They characteristically wake early in the morning and can't go back to sleep again. They also find falling asleep difficult and are restless and easily awakened. What sleep they do get is not refreshing. Disturbing dreams in which trapped feelings seek expression often interrupt their sleep.

The depressed person appears harried, worried, desperate to contain his anger and self-hate. To tolerate this state for long is exhausting. Defenses wear down and in the worst cases energy stops flowing outward at all. When people feel helpless to contain their rage and believe that things won't improve, they may turn their anger against themselves in one final attempt to end their plain—either as a cry for help or as a real attempt to end their life.

But a depression isn't always without its positive side. Even though a depression is painful to endure, it also can lower defenses that have been too rigid or too obscuring and permit a person a clearer, less distorted view of himself. During a depression people frequently begin to understand themselves for the first time and may be put in touch with other self-revealing feelings. In depression a person has a sense of having lost something very important that he was previously unaware of.

He may feel that he has lost so much already that he has nothing more to lose by being honest with himself and reexamining what he thinks is important in his life.

A depression, if accompanied by this kind of new awareness, may be the turning point for someone who previously has been poorly organized and not able to find direction. The collapse of the defenses can help a person to reshape his life, to find the courage to challenge what he thought was so important before — "If what I had was supposed to be so important to me, why wasn't I happy?" He may realize there is still time to change. Many people finally stop taking life for granted after overcoming a depression.

Becoming depressed is hardly recommended as the ideal way for finding out what you're really like, but to ignore the realities about yourself that are revealed when your defenses are down is to miss a valuable opportunity to grow. Worse, the old anger over loss stays trapped, unsolved, and all your suffering has been for nothing. There is, after all, no inherent virtue in pain. It needs to be used.

Unsolved depressive feelings can begin to interfere with a person's ability to work or live. When the pain is too great, insight is often slight. Help is needed. There are various kinds of treatment available, each with its own merits and drawbacks. The method used depends on the type and severity of the disorder and should be undertaken under the care of a professional.

Treatment of depression by psychotherapy involves helping a person release his trapped anger and keep it from building up further. Often the therapist plays the role of a "safe" person the patient can be angry at without adding to his guilt.

Electroshock is a physical form of therapy. It creates a partial amnesia that strengthens the defense of denial by which the depressed person has tried unsuccessfully to contain his anger. This artificially induced forgetfulness helps suppress the anger and guilt the patient has been unable to deny. It may help the patient with psychotic depression feel better momentarily, but it leaves him with less of himself to work with because of the partial memory loss. Frequently when the effects of the electroshock wear off the patient becomes depressed again. Electroshock therapy can also make it more difficult for psychotherapy to work later on because it interferes with one's ability to remember and resolve painful feelings.

Like psychotherapy and electroshock, the treatment of depression with anti-depressant medication is only partially effective and works with some patients and not with others. The effectivenss of anti-depressant drugs is often psychological—beginning with the doctor. It gives the doctor something tangible to treat a patient with, and he thereby may tend to project a more confident attitude, which in turn may help the patient believe in him. But too many drugs are given these days.

An anti-depressant, Imipramine, has been shown to increase the amount of anger expressed in a depressed patient's dreams, which then gradually decreases as the patient improves. This suggests that some of the improvement with this medication may be the result of depleting through dreams the pool of anger that has been fueling the patient's guilt and depression. Chlordiazepoxide, a widely used tranquilizer, seems to increase the anxiety expressed in patients' dreams — dreams that in this way apparently allow the patient to express feelings forbidden elsewhere.

Generally, both doctors and patients rely too much on medicine and technology and too little on humanness and the understanding of how feelings work. In depression, as mentioned, going to the depths of your feelings and seeing your inner world as it is may allow you to make decisions you were totally incapable of making before. People recovering from depression often are able to say, "I've been punished enough by my own feelings, now it's time for me to do something for myself. I know what's making me miserable and I know I can't go on living my life the way I have been. That would make me a phony, a fake. I don't want to spend the rest of my life pretending I should be happy fulfilling someone else's wishes for me. I don't want to spend the rest of my life trying to correct the uncorrectable mistakes of my past. I want to live the life that's mine."

People think thoughts like this all the time but often feel too guilty to take a positive step in their own best interests. Depression can let us see that we're responsible for our own lives and must take charge of fulfilling ourselves. No one is going to do it for us. If we don't take care of ourselves first we're useless to ourselves and to others.

Adolescents often feel depressed, because, as suggested earlier, their views of themselves are constantly changing and they continually suffer lapses in self-esteem. But these lapses can also become the rallying point for growth and for correcting their mistakes—for giving up artificial and childish ways of acting just to be one of the boys, or girls, at the expense of being themselves.

In a way, a depression makes us all adolescents again, with all of the potential and opportunity for growing once more. A depression tells us there is something wrong with the way we're dealing with the world, that there is something wrong with the way we're leading our lives. The pain of depression often makes it possible for us to grow again and to give up sacrificing unnecessarily for others.

Not being your best self is painful. To accept the responsibility of your own feelings and to decide to find what is best in you is the best legacy of a depression.

To be your best self means that you become honest with your feelings. That you give up expectations of being perfect and therefore the need to conceal what you feel, because what you feel is you.

Being your *best* self means that the unique mixture of feelings that is you is the best possible way you can be no matter what those feelings happen to be.

It is best to accept a depression as proof that you are real and that you care. Accept that you are basically good even if sometimes you doubt it and, what's more, can offer evidence to back up your opinion. The problem is not that you are bad, but that you feel that you are bad and that this self-prejudice has caused you to become lost in your guilt.

Take courage to grow again.

CHAPTER SEVEN

Getting Out of Emotional Debt and Becoming Open

ONCE YOU'VE learned to understand your feelings and to be open and honest in expressing them, you can become free of the emotional debts of your past and increasingly clear in your perception of the world. Once you're free of the need to distort and have no preconceived expectations of reality, life becomes uncomplicated. The present moment — now — seems to become elongated as you become ever more available to yourself and to the people you care about. Life becomes fuller because it's more fully experienced. Whereas once you avoided pain and shut off part of the world to contain it, now you're free to feel all your hurts and losses, settle them, and move on to the next moment in life with minimal baggage from the past. Most important, once out of emotional debt, you're into yourself, into really knowing yourself. It's easier to make decisions that are in your best interest, to shape your life so it allows you the greatest opportunity for reaching your full potential. Without honesty in the acceptance of your feelings, followed by their understanding, none of this would be possible.

We all get into emotional debt from time to time. Emotional debt is a condition of imbalance in which feelings are trapped instead of expressed. I've stressed that keeping feelings from being expressed naturally employs defenses and drains energy. The more feelings are held in, the less energy you have to be yourself and the less free you become. If you're in emotional debt either your feelings will eventually escape in the wrong direction or your defenses will become so rigid that you can't interact spontaneously. Your world will seem either frantic or full, out of control or joyless. It will be a projection of your locked-in past — not your outgoing present. It will be a distortion.

Getting out of emotional debt is less complicated than it sounds. We remain trapped by unexpressed feelings from our past partly because we're afraid to express those feelings, and partly because we don't understand how feelings work. If you can understand how feelings flow in response to loss— and by now I hope you can—and are able to accept your anger at being hurt, you're already on the high road out of emotional debt. It's when hurt and anger aren't expressed honestly that emotional debt is piled up in the first place.

The first step in getting out of emotional debt is to allow yourself to feel whatever you feel without making a value judgment. Don't *try* to feel, simply *feel*. Don't be afraid to feel because you think a particular emotion will show you in an unfavorable light. Your feelings can tell you a great deal about the world and yourself, but they shouldn't be considered evidence to prove your worth. Just because you have angry feelings doesn't make you a "bad" person, nor do altruistic feelings necessarily make you a "good" person.

To get out of emotional debt you need to accept yourself, your humanness, including shortcomings. You need to accept the idea that imperfect as you are you're still worthwhile and that you and your feelings matter. You have to take responsibility for your feelings and learn to love yourself enough to act on them. This means that if you feel something, you need to have the courage to express it. How can you possibly grow if you don't admit to your own feelings and take responsibility for them? You can't fix feelings you don't own up to.

Letting out feelings can certainly be frightening, for it's in the arena of the feelings that people tend to feel least in control and so most fearful. It's also at the point where we reject our own feelings that we erect our defenses, and if we allow them to become entrenched they put a wall between us and our feelings. When we're too distant from our feelings, then any feeling that gets through, no matter how small or ordinary, has the capacity to throw us off balance, to confuse and even immobilize. People who are massively defended against their feelings use up all of their energy just to stay intact. They dread feeling anything. It's hard enough just to get up in the morning. They tend to be more afraid of their feelings than of the events that cause them, and so they do little to resolve their problems. Instead, they waste their energies trying to convince others that they're not afraid or hurt or angry or sad: "No, really, I'm fine . . . of course I'm okay . . . who said I look sad? . . . what do you mean? . . . just leave me alone, *please* . . ." If they allowed themselves at least to begin to express their hurt or anger as they felt them, the stockpile would be reduced, as well as the accompanying defensiveness and stress.

People burdened with withheld emotions are usually under continual stress, covering up as they are for something *they* think is unacceptable. Their emotional life is so guarded they don't see the world as it is. They think it's the world outside that's got them so tense and nervous, when actually the trouble originates within—where, so long as it stays unacknowledged, it also remains unrelieved.

To get out of emotional debt you need to believe neither you nor the world will come unstuck if you give expression to your feelings —

expressing feelings appropriately rarely leads to losing control. Getting angry and crying, for example, is not being out of control but merely expressing intense feelings. Some people don't think it's "nice" to have such strong feelings. Such a notion of what's nice is itself stifling. The very fear of losing control often can result from denying the urge to let out feelings. The trapped feelings only build up to trip off arguments, explosions, and magnify hurts out of proportion. And all of this tends to give the inhibited person the impression he's out of control—which in a way, by *his* lights, he is. The sensation of *any* feelings being expressed, somehow getting through his Maginot Line of defenses, comes as a surprise and tends to unnerve him. "My God ... what's happening to me ..." might be his terrified reaction. The answer, of course, is ... "Nothing, except what comes naturally." Yes, the answer may be easy, but accepting it for such a person isn't. Sympathy and understanding are needed.

Getting out of emotional debt and staying open—they're the objectives for all of us who want to free ourselves from the crippling burden of unreal expectations born in our past. No matter how terrible your past life has been or how rigid your upbringing, there's plenty of basis to hope for growth if you can learn to accept your feelings and stop apologizing for them. If you can't even be free to feel what you feel, you're in bondage regardless of the freedom of the society you live in. Hippie commune or Beacon Hill flat—feelings rule the roost. Whoever finds you unacceptable because you express them is a person who doesn't want you to be real—you can probably do without him.

The happy consequence of getting free of burdensome emotions is to become open. To be open you need to understand what you feel, know where the feeling comes from, and be able to express that feeling to whomever is appropriate. In solving problems you can now rely on your feelings to indicate the right direction. The intellect and its tool, logic, can be led astray. They need the active collaboration of your feelings to keep them from altering reality to suit false needs. Feelings tell the truth. When you are open, needs still exist, but you can perceive them clearly because you are open to your feelings that define and interpret them.

Being open is to be in continuous contact with the world around you through your feelings. You are continually rising to a higher, unencumbered level of perceiving the world, with a view that is less and less defensive. As you become open you depend less on what others say and more on your own sense of the world—on what your feelings say.

When you are open you're less anxious. You need only to stop and ask: What am I afraid of losing? What is threatening me now? How may I be hurt? Am I in some sort of danger? Am I afraid

of accepting some part of myself? Am I afraid of
assuming responsibility for doing something that
hurt another person? Am I afraid of taking and
handling blame for some act or word because of
the feeling of guilt? As you ask, with an understanding of the relevant feelings and how they
operate, and free of the weight of emotional debt,
you can answer your questions near-automatically
to resolve your anxiety — the more frequently
asked, the more easily and automatically answered.
If you exercise your muscles they're toned and
behave more efficiently for you. If you train your
mind on hard problems you make it a more effi-
cient tool as well. In similar fashion, if your feelings are operating freely your emotional health,
well-being and personal development have got to
respond to this openness.

That voice of your inner feelings speaks for the
you that has the greatest chance of making a success
of your life with the least wasted effort. You don't
need to create this person because you already *are*
this person. It's only your defenses that stand in the
way of expressing this higher self in you. Once
expressed, it can be refined and shaped further,
but it's there or it isn't from the start.

There are no great mysteries in life really, just
doors to open to explore each step in your growth.
Each new step is taken with a little pain. Just as it
takes some energy to block an emotion, so it takes
energy to free one. Even if you know what's block-
ing your progress, you can't grow until you give up

the defenses that are holding you in place. Giving up defenses allows you to see yourself as you are. This can be frightening, but it's necessary if you really want to move on to the next step. Each step is taken by experiencing openly and honestly the feelings that have previously been concealed.

The way to discovering the truth begins with being honest with your feelings. To be honest means to state the highest truth as you see it without apology or defense, without pretense or selectivity. To bombard other people with painful revelations about themselves may be telling the "truth," but only a selected part of it. The greater truth may be that you are merely being hurtful out of a sense of anger that you may not be expressing appropriately. The highest honesty is seeking beyond your own distortions without illusions.

Feelings without honesty are defenses
The world without honesty is an illusion
Memory without honesty is only a fantasy
Time without honesty can never be now
Space without honesty can never be here
Love without honesty is possessiveness.

•

Without honesty there is no real growth
Without honesty there is no freedom
Without honesty there is no hope
Without honesty nothing is real
Without honesty nothing is.

When people become honest they can begin to experience the same reality. When two people share the same reality they not only validate their individual lives but life itself. With honesty not only our sense of reality grows but so does our strength and self-acceptance, reinforced by others who are on the same journey.

The journey begins the same way for all of us, by asking ourselves with as much honesty as possible, along with new understanding: "What do I feel? Where is that feeling coming from? Is it familiar? In what way? When did it occur before? What event is linked to it? Is that event a threat of a loss, an actual loss, or a hurt, or some other feeling? You know now that the feeling of anxiety will usually be attached to the threat of a loss, that sometimes just remembering an old loss can re-create the original anxiety. Usually this means you haven't yet completely accepted the loss and that your anxiety can't be settled until the loss is totally accepted and your grief is allowed to surface. You also know that if the event recalled involves hurt, the blocked feeling is almost always anger. Allowing the anger out is the way to clear the persistent feeling of hurt. And if the painful event involves much anger there is likely to be recollections both of hurt and guilt over the anger. Again, the way to clear these feelings is to accept the loss and hurt, and to express the anger.

There's no mystique to this method. Any sentient, normal person can use it, and intelligence quotient is not the determining factor—indeed, if it were the majority of us would be in considerable difficulty. How often have you or a friend sat down to "figure out" a problem, and come up empty, blank? Still as uncomfortable as before? It's only when our feelings—our sixth sense—are allowed play, and when we are able to pay meaningful attention to them, that the discomfort diminishes and we're able to go about our lives with renewed efficiency and pleasure. When we're emotionally uncomfortable we're least likely to function at our best, regardless of our intelligence. None of this, of course, is to suggest a kind of anti-intellectual mindlessness. It is to re-emphasize that thinking a problem through without feeling it through is to reach at best a partial, temporary and superficial solution. It's a matter of what works.

As you become open, you also become much more aware of your so-called intuition. You can "sense" more about other people because you can receive what comes from them to you without distorting it with your defenses. See for yourself how this can work by trying the following exercise. Sit quietly for five minutes alone in a room with your eyes closed and clear your mind of previous images and thoughts. Let it go blank. Concentrate on the images behind your eyes. Arrange to have a second person enter the room without speaking. Open your eyes. You will experience a "sense" of the other person by perceiving his presence as a subtle change in your feelings.

Such a perception occurs every time two people meet, whether or not they notice it. It results from the interaction of the energies of the two people, each with its own particular force and quality. You may notice a vague sense of warmth or coldness, of power or vulnerability. The change you perceive is the emotional "aura" of the other person. It varies and changes in a person just as his feelings do. A person's aura tells something important about him. There's nothing especially new about this phenomenon. Everybody has, for example, felt threatened at some point by the mere presence of a menacing person, even when he says nothing. There's nothing especially mystical in this. We're talking about the equipment that's within every human being. It doesn't depend on occult training to perceive it. It depends on *you*, developing toward your fullest potential as a feeling and therefore knowing person.

If you practice "sensing" this way, you can learn to develop your perception and intuition to a high degree of consciousness. When you learn to sense things in others, you will also learn to sense more more in yourself, you will also learn to sense more in others. Feelings you were formerly unaware of are lowered. Once you learn to be at this place where intellect and feelings meet, you can enjoy the constant interplay of the two. It becomes easier for you to tell what is real. Your skill at this, as at any other art, improves and sharpens with practice.

When you learn to sense in this way, you will be in touch with a new source of wisdom — the truth of your own experience, which is now made available to you. You become a reliable instrument by which to measure the input from the outside world. When something makes you feel uncertain, you're probably right to feel so and need only say, "I'm not sure," and ask somebody for an explanation or for further time to consider whatever the situation or statement is. If what somebody says sounds to you like an excuse, a defense, or doesn't feel real or honest, say so and say it directly. If another person is pressuring you into something, tell him so. You'll likely get a good or at least a real response from him because your interpretation of his behavior is accurate and he'll know it, whether he wants to admit it or not. You give him feedback, let him know realistically the effect of his behavior on you and open the way for a dialogue, beginning with your asking questions about why he's pressuring you, why he won't let you go at your own pace . . . It's no longer attack-react-attack but an exchange based on your accurate perception of reality — a perception you've managed because you are open to his feelings and to yours. You don't need to prove what you feel; you only need to know what you feel and to communicate it.

It's almost always self-defeating to conceal the

truth of what you experience from yourself. A person who thinks there are things he shouldn't talk about or feel would do well to re-examine why he is so guarded. People are supposed to talk about feelings. It's bad enough to have a conversation with somebody who can't or won't let through what he feels about you. If you're both in the avoidance business, the exchange becomes artificial and stilted. You might as well punch it out on a computer card. The trouble is, these unspoken feelings generally surface in some form at some other and less appropriate time anyway, causing great mischief, confusion and probably further defensiveness.

When you're open your feelings direct and inform your mental process. They quickly alert you to a situation that doesn't *feel* right. It's then that you need to slow down and ask, "What's wrong here?" If possible, it's helpful to share your reaction with somebody else. You're not perfect, or infallible, but if you've managed through understanding to become open you've got a very reasonable basis for believing more often than not that your view is a clear one.

When you're open and alert each person, each impression makes its full and unique impact on your experience and consciousness. If you have learned how feelings work, you'll be able to understand and handle the behavior of others — whether, for example, they're hurting you out of anger, or trying to make you believe you hurt them so they can avoid their own feeling of guilt.

Being open also means your sexual energy is freely available to you. For the average person this is surely vital—most of us can't exist at the exalted level of sex sublimated in great works that has been ascribed to some great artists. The problems that get in the way of expressing and enjoying sexuality are rarely specifically sexual—they're all the problems with expressing feelings that have already been discussed. If you feel good about yourself as a person, if you're open and free with your feelings, you should have little difficulty enjoying a full sexual life. Problems in technique are generally minor. Few things improve your sexual performance and ability to enjoy sex as much as improving the way you feel about yourself.

This book has tried to help you answer some fundamental questions in your life:

Who are you?

How did you get that way?

Where are you going?

The road to each person's highest self is paved by feelings honestly perceived and straightforwardly expressed. Each of us must try to create the best life we can imagine for ourselves by tying together the most promising pieces of our past with our best sense of our present and future.

Only you know your dream for yourself. Only

you can make it happen. Only you know the person inside you. Your goal is to let him out.

To get to that goal you will have to become as open and honest about your feelings as you possibly can, letting them flow, taking responsibility for them—for your life; they are the best, most direct way to discovering the true and real person inside you. Along the way you will find yourself becoming free of emotional debt to the past. You will be able to be yourself without exaggeration or apology.

You will, in the best sense, have arrived.

Afterword

A PERSON who does not understand the feelings beneath his actions doesn't really understand himself at all. He spends his life trapped in a world full of dark corners where silent forces out of his control influence his actions and direct him.

Our feelings define reality for us more directly and more completely than anything else. Our feelings define time for us: A loss in the future is perceived as fear. A loss in the present is felt as pain. A loss in the past is experienced as anger. Our feelings center the world and make it accessible to us. Without feelings the world is remote.

Life should be lived in the present, for it is only in the present that we're able to exert any control over our lives. We can't change our past and the future is continually formed in the present. We need to learn to invest our energy in the present, where it will do the most good. If we take care of the present honestly and without pretense or apology, the future will take care of itself.

All the creations of man's genius and acts of

compassion over the centuries, while pointing to his promise, don't change the fact that he's forever stuck with a finite mind in an infinite system. His highest sense, his creative sense, while it may have provided him with some intimation of immortality by allowing him to create things that outlive him, seems to have offered him little in finding a way to bridge the gap between his intellectual limitations and the infinite forces working on him. Perhaps this gap can never be closed. Perhaps no one can ever really comprehend the cosmos or understand why we were made aware of our journey through it. Nonetheless, we're alive because we feel life, and ought to take care to preserve what gifts we've been allowed.

If we can't comprehend the greater world, we can focus our attention on the world within, the world of feelings, and establish an order and understanding there. If we can feel and be ourselves and permit our feelings to flow where they seemed naturally inclined, we will find ourselves better people—by being the best of ourselves.

Perhaps this, after all, is the best we can aspire to, to be our best selves. In the freedom of being our best we can allow other people to be whatever they are. We assume responsibility for our lives and act on our feelings, doing what feels right to us, making the important decisions in our lives in our own enlightened self-interest. It is only after we each insure our own survival that we can freely help others in a way not determined by our own needs. Greed is seldom seen in people who have fulfilled themselves.

To be rich is to need nothing. It is impossible to acquire everything, though some people still vainly try, but sadly too few people are willing to take the risk of becoming their best selves, to discover who they really are and use their feelings as their best guide in that search.

Each of us has the right to take his own life seriously and to discover what it was that he was designed by nature to do. If everyone followed the suggestions of his inner "voice," his world would change very much for the better. So, I suspect, would the world outside.

If we each used our feelings as a guide to reach the path for becoming our highest selves, we would at least be on the way to finding fulfillment in our own life, and the greater world would begin to make sense. A person who is not comprehensible to himself cannot expect to experience a world that makes much sense.

If each person followed his feelings, he would find the direction he is really looking for—without dogma, cult, government or guru.

The light you are seeking is inside.
The light is life, is love, is you.
Find it, nurture it, share it.
To seek it is to take part in the infinite.